# GARDEN *to* GARDEN

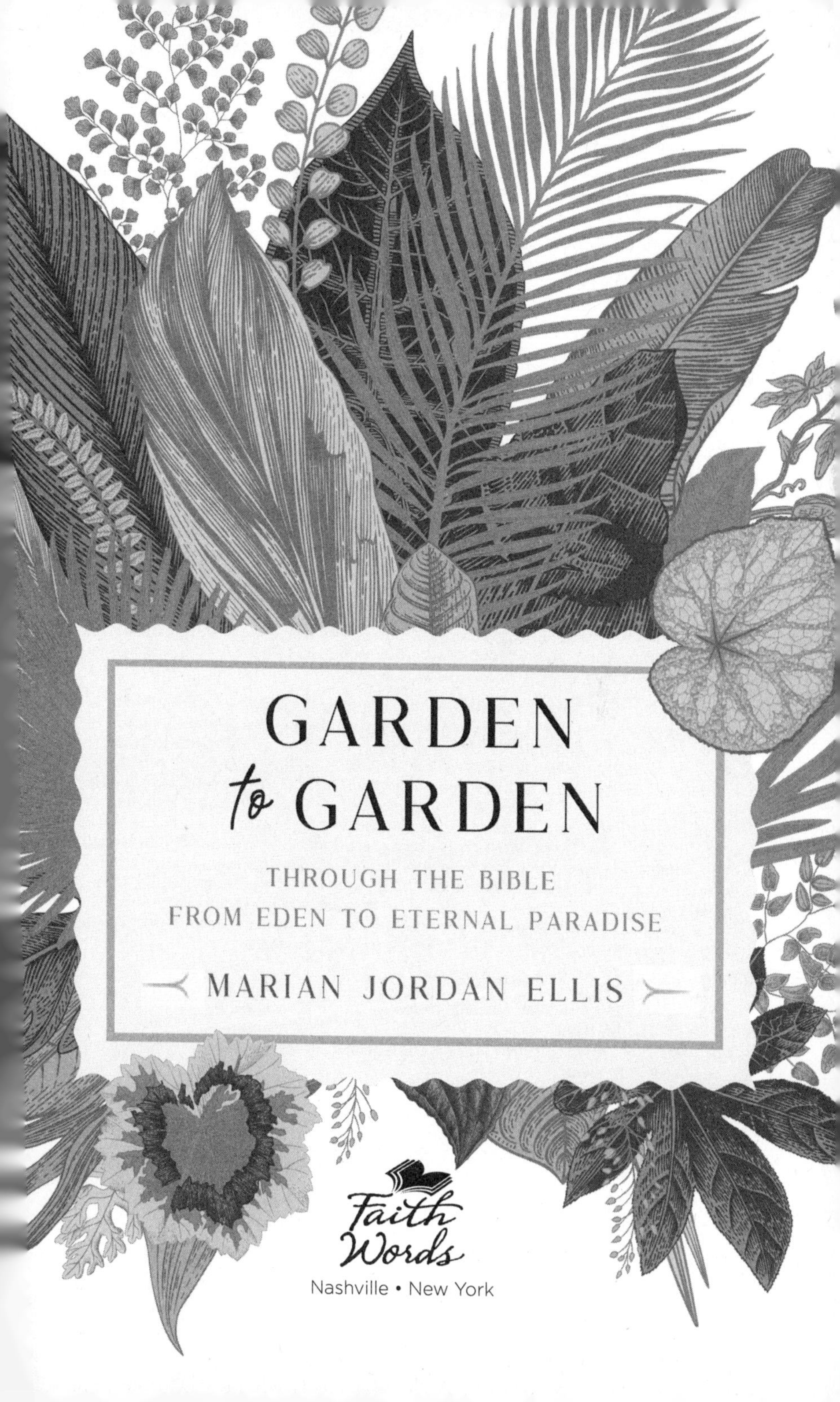

# GARDEN *to* GARDEN

THROUGH THE BIBLE
FROM EDEN TO ETERNAL PARADISE

MARIAN JORDAN ELLIS

Faith Words
Nashville • New York

FaithWords
Hachette Book Group
1290 Avenue of the Americas, New York, NY 10104
faithwords.com
twitter.com/faithwords

First Edition: February 2024

FaithWords is a division of Hachette Book Group, Inc. The FaithWords name and logo are trademarks of Hachette Book Group, Inc.



Print book interior design by Bart Dawson

Library of Congress Cataloging-in-Publication Data
Names: Jordan, Marian L., author.
Title: Garden to garden : through the bible from Eden to eternal paradise / Marian Jordan Ellis.
Description: First edition. | New York, NY : FaithWords, 2024.
Identifiers: LCCN 2023036590 | ISBN 9781546004509 (hardcover) | ISBN 9781546004516 (ebook)
Subjects: LCSH: Bible—Commentaries. | Bible stories. | Devotional calendars.
Classification: LCC BS491.3 .J67 2024 | DDC 220.7—dc23/eng/20230928
LC record available at https://lccn.loc.gov/2023036590

ISBNs: 978-1-5460-0450-9 (hardcover); 978-1-5460-0451-6 (ebook)

Printed in the United States of America

LSC-C

Printing 1, 2023

*To Justin, my beloved*

# CONTENTS

## Emmanuel



## Eternity

# INTRODUCTION

## From Eden to Eternity

As you embark on this journey to discover how the Bible unfolds from garden to garden, begin by imagining you've stepped into a theater. Your hands are loaded with popcorn and M&Ms, and you find your seat only to realize you've arrived in the middle of the movie. People around you are engrossed in the drama. Some are crying, and others sit in anticipation at the edge of their seats. Puzzled, you look at your ticket and realize the movie began an hour earlier and you've missed half of it. Now, you have questions:

*Who's that woman?*

*Why is everyone sad?*

*Why are they afraid of that guy?*

*Where did the dragon come from?*

*Who's the dude with the sword?*

When I first started following Jesus, this is how I experienced the Bible. Honestly, I felt lost. I knew only fragments of the story. I'd heard about Jesus and was familiar with some names like David, Moses, and Mary, but truthfully, I had no idea how those biblical characters were connected, or the part they played in the great redemption story. So, whenever I read my Bible, although dramatic and inspiring, I didn't grasp the grand narrative of the Bible.

The Bible is one story, which unfolds from garden to garden. While it contains sixty-six individual books written over thousands of years, it reveals one unified message because there is one Divine Author behind it all. From the Garden of Eden in Genesis to the eternal garden paradise promised in Revelation, the Bible explains how God redeems humanity from sin and death and makes all things new!

But unlike a fairy tale or a Hollywood movie, this story is supernatural in origin. Scripture is God-breathed. Opening its pages, we discover who we are, why we are here, what happened to us, and our eternal destiny. What is most amazing is that through the Bible we come to know the Author. It's from reading the Word that we learn of God's redeeming love and His unconquerable grace.

This Bible has rightly been called God's love story. Like all great stories, the Bible tells us of a rescue mission where Love does the unimaginable to rescue the beloved. It is a tale of brokenness and beauty, groaning and grace, heartbreak and healing, and of course, a conquering Hero.

Who is the Hero of this story? While He was foretold throughout the Old Testament, our Savior stepped into the human story two thousand years ago, and the world knows Him by the name of Jesus Christ. The Hero of humanity is Jesus the Messiah, who was crucified on a Roman cross but conquered Satan, sin, and death by rising from the grave.

Although the weeds of sin, shame, and blame grow wild in the human heart, the longing for Eden, our true home, always remains. We were created for something glorious, something beautiful, something distinguished by the Presence of God.

In *Garden to Garden*, you will discover how God moved through human history to restore us to His Presence. The Word of God is one unified story that promises and points to the Redeemer, Jesus Christ. From the dawn of creation to the dramatic New

Creation of the heavens and earth, there is the one Eternal God, whom we will come to know as the Great I AM, working His sovereign plan to redeem and restore that which was lost. The God who created us to dwell with Him in Eden's paradise is the One who comes to our rescue and makes all things new.

# AUTHOR'S NOTE

*Garden to Garden* is a journey through the Bible from Eden to eternity. Over the next thirty days, you will see how the whole Bible fits together as one story. Each daily reading is divided into four parts:

## SEED

This is your focal passage for the day. Take your time to read the passage slowly and focus on the key words, phrases, and images. Keep in mind that all Scripture is God-breathed, and He spoke these words to reveal His heart, to enrich your relationship with Him, and to give you encouragement, instruction, and direction for each day.

## CULTIVATE

Reading these suggested Scripture passages in your own Bible will provide the greater context of your SEED passage and deepen your understanding of God's Word. As you CULTIVATE a daily habit of reading the Bible, you will find the roots of your faith growing deeper and deeper.

## FLOURISH

This devotional commentary will connect the larger redemption story of the Bible and help you discover how God's Word applies to your life today. Through these daily readings, the grand narrative of the Bible will become clearer.

## ⤙ HARVEST

A garden is cultivated to produce a harvest. It is the Lord who is the Divine Gardener of our souls, and as we yield to the work of His hands, we are transformed. As we sit in God's Presence and study His Word, the Holy Spirit plants the Seed in our hearts, which produces the fruit of the Spirit. These HARVEST reflection questions are designed for you to process with the Lord. Grab your journal and set aside time to sit with the Lord, allowing the Holy Spirit to tend the soil of your heart and produce a harvest of righteousness as you answer these HARVEST questions.

# THE INVITATION

The primary purpose of this book is to enhance your knowledge of God's Word and provide you with a greater understanding of the redemption story and how it threads together from garden to garden. But as lofty as those goals are, I want to caution you against engaging with this from merely an intellectual posture without engaging your heart.

The Bible is divine revelation. From Genesis to Revelation, the Lord God Almighty speaks to us, declaring who He is and what He has done to restore us to His glorious Presence. This is an invitation from King Jesus, who says:

> *Behold, I stand at the door and knock. If anyone hears my voice and opens the door, I will come in to him and eat with him, and he with me.*
>
> —Revelation 3:20 ESV

My sincere desire is for you to encounter the Lord God who walked in the Garden of Eden, who invites you to return to His Presence, and who longs for you to flourish in His marvelous light. This is a holy invitation to know and be known by the Living God. As you begin this journey, I want to impart to you the soul-stirring words of A. W. Tozer. His words contain my prayer for you, the pilgrim on this journey:

> For it is not mere words that nourish the soul, but God Himself, and unless and until the hearers find God in personal experience they are not the better for having heard the truth. The Bible is not an end in itself, but a means to bring men (and women) to an intimate and satisfying knowledge of God, that they may enter into Him, that they may delight in His presence, may taste and know the inner sweetness of the very God Himself in the core and center of their hearts.[1]

Friend, I pray *Garden to Garden* leads you deep into the heart of God to behold His goodness and experience His nearness. May the lavish love of the Father, the grace of the Lord Jesus, and the inspiration of the Holy Spirit be with you.

For His Glory,
Marian

---

1 A. W. Tozer, *The Pursuit of God* (Shawnee, KS: Gideon House Books, 2017), 10.

# GARDEN *to* GARDEN

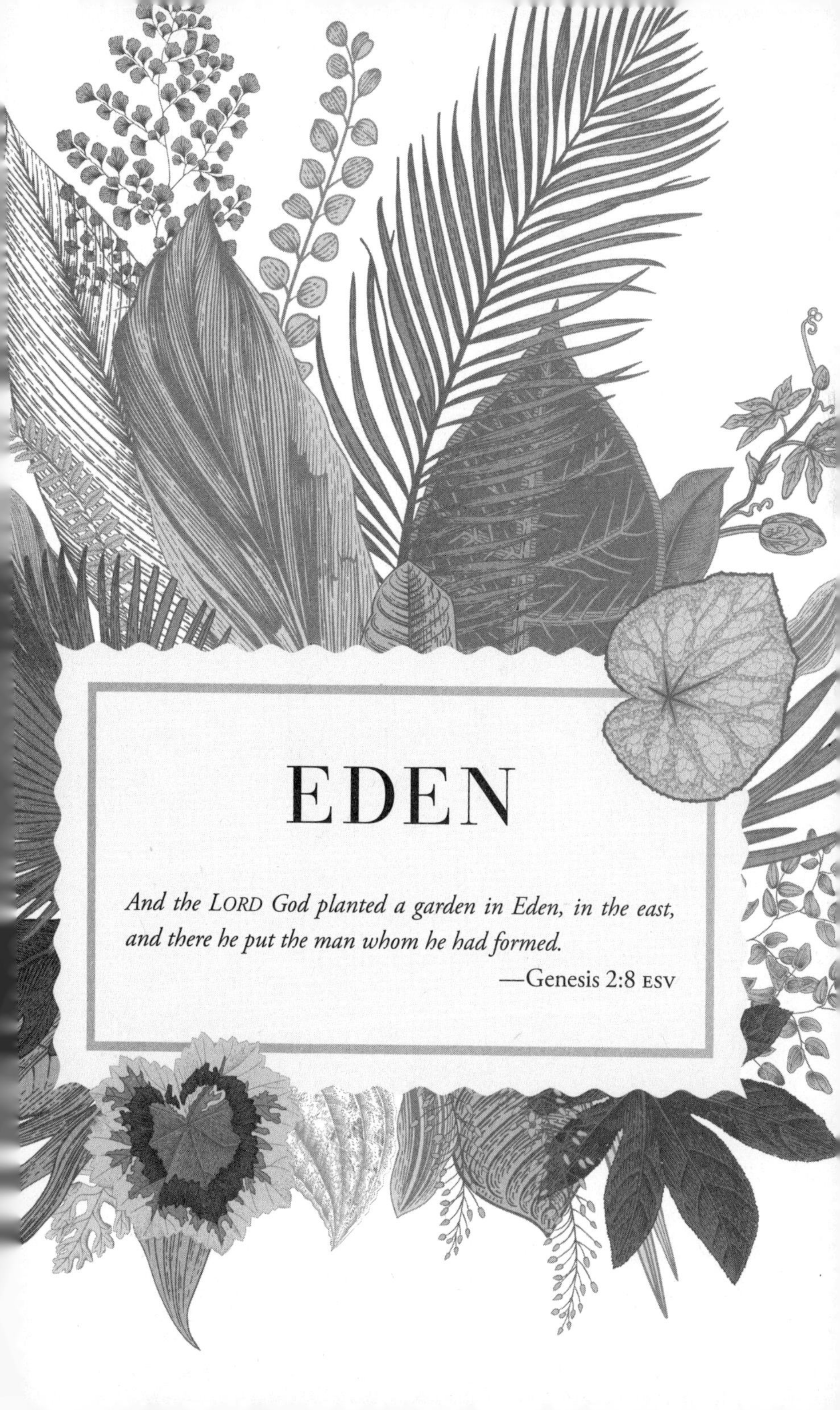

# EDEN

*And the* LORD *God planted a garden in Eden, in the east, and there he put the man whom he had formed.*

—Genesis 2:8 ESV

DAY 1

# THE GOD OF THE GARDEN

## SEED

*In the beginning, God created the heavens and the earth.*

—Genesis 1:1 ESV

## CULTIVATE

Read Genesis 1; Psalm 16.

## FLOURISH

One morning while vacationing at the beach, I woke up early to watch the sunrise over the ocean and spend time with God. I had awakened with this tugging in my heart, drawing me out of the comfort of my bed, to come away by myself and meet with the Lord.

With my Bible tucked under my arm, I walked down to the shore without knowing the revelation that awaited me. At that time, I was new to the Christian faith. I loved Jesus and was hungry to know Him more. But honestly, I came to faith with a lot of baggage.

My baggage was the false beliefs I held about the character of God. I grew up in a religious culture built on rules and behavior modification, where God was angry and aloof. And since I had been the poster child for rebellion, I was certain God would be mad at all the ways I had failed. I had no idea that my perception of God was false and didn't align with how He is revealed in Scripture. But thankfully, as I came to know Jesus and began comprehending God's grace, those deep-rooted lies were exposed and started falling away.

This brings me back to the beach when God spoke to me from His Word. Watching the crystal-blue water sparkle with the first rays of sunlight, I opened my Bible and read:

> *Delight yourself in the LORD, and he will give you the desires of your heart.*
>
> —Psalm 37:4 ESV

Delight. Watching the sunrise by the ocean while communing with God pretty much defines "delight" for me. Hands down, the best part of that morning was the peace of His Presence. Friends, there's absolutely no substitute for God's peace. I should know, because before Jesus, my life was characterized by chaos and emptiness. This state was due to the consequences of my choices and the darkness I lived in. But as I sat before the Lord that morning, I felt whole, alive, and loved. The crashing waves carried echoes of Eden.

At that time, I didn't know much about the Garden of Eden, but in the beauty of that sunrise I felt connected to God in a way I had never felt before. The Bible calls this state *shalom*, which means "peace, wholeness, and soundness." Shalom is the state of spiritual and emotional wholeness that comes when our souls are right with God, when our hearts are at peace in His Presence, and when we are at rest in the goodness of our Heavenly Father. This was one of my first tastes of shalom, but I was hungry for more.

As the sun peeked over the horizon, I continued to meditate on the Scripture and read, "Delight yourself in the LORD..." The truth dawned on me: That's the relationship the Lord wants with us. Not rules or religion, but one where we enjoy His Presence and delight in Him. A relationship with God is not just a cliché that Christians use; this is the very existence we are invited to enjoy.

And as I continued to read, I saw this promise attached to the invitation: When you delight in Him, He "will give you the desires of your heart." As I chewed upon this promise, I sensed God whisper a question: *Marian, what do you desire?*

God invited me to share my heart. This is intimacy with God, a relationship where we know Him and are known by Him. God is a good Father who loves His children and wants to bless us with His goodness.

Unfortunately, I didn't know or trust this truth about God's heart at the time, so in response to the question "What do you desire?" my answer was unfiltered and raw. I blurted out, "Like You care!" (Yep, you read that right.) I didn't conjure up a good church-girl reply. From deep in my heart a lie I believed about God was exposed: I didn't believe God loved or cared for me, and my honest response tumbled out before I had time to stop it. Startled by my own transparency and fearful that I had offended God, I covered my mouth with my hand and ducked my head.

The Lord didn't strike me down for my honesty. God is so gracious. Looking back, I know the Lord woke me up, nudged me out of bed, and invited me down to that beach just so we could have that little heart-to-heart.

God's question led to some soul-searching. *Why did I believe God didn't care about me? Where did that response come from?* As I dug my toes into the sand, I felt the Lord digging into my heart, exposing and removing a lie about His character: the lie that said, "God is not good." Sure, I believed God was real—I wasn't an atheist. But I didn't think He was good. I'd believed the lie that was as old as time. And that blatant assault on God's character kept me from fully trusting Him and experiencing the abundant life *with Him*. The truth is this: I had never experienced shalom before because I didn't really know the truth about God.

God loved me too much to let that lie fester. Therefore, the Lord used His truth to set me free. Over the next few years, I began consuming Scripture like oxygen. It became my lifeline. And as I did, my mind was renewed to see God rightly. I came to relate to King David's words like they were my own testimony:

> *I say to the LORD, "You are my Lord;*
> *I have no good apart from you."...*
> *You make known to me the path of life;*
> *in your presence there is fullness of joy;*
> *at your right hand are pleasures forevermore.*
>
> —Psalm 16:2; 11 ESV

Indeed, in His Presence is the fullness of joy. Right there we are told where to find the very thing this world is craving—joy. It can't be bottled and it can't be bought; it can be found only in His Presence. In the Bible we are given directions to the Source of shalom and the One who reveals to us the path of life.

Perhaps you are reading this and are skeptical. I get it. Since we live in a world characterized by fake news, it's a challenge to know what to believe sometimes. That's why we need an authoritative source to reveal truth. In this world proliferated with lies, the Bible stands as the authoritative truth for us, and it begins on page one by telling us the ultimate truth that we all need to know: We are created by God and for God.

Like any good book, the Bible opens in Genesis 1:1 by revealing the Star of the story: *"In the beginning God created the heavens and the earth."* God stands at the center of all the glory that unfolds. Genesis reveals that God spoke and all things came into existence.

He is the Master of Molecules and by the power of His word, He created something out of nothing. God said, "Let there be...," and He brought forth light, water, sun, moon, land, vegetation, and a kaleidoscope of creatures to inhabit His creation. While we aren't given the physics, chemistry, or biology of this creation process, we are told the Source.

The first two chapters of Genesis describe the creation of the world. Scripture tells us that God was pleased with all He made, that He repeatedly described it as "good." In these chapters, we discover God's original desire for creation. He created a beautiful garden where harmony existed between nature and humans, ample food was provided for our enjoyment, and men and women were given creative work to do with God and for His glory. But most importantly, humans lived with God and enjoyed a relationship with Him. The Garden of Eden is a picture of true shalom.

But back to the Star of the story. Who is the One who commands such power to simply speak and the universe is formed? In the original language, the title of God is "Elohim," the infinite, all-powerful Creator and sustainer of the world. With breathtaking brevity, the Bible reveals the origin of life, but we also learn our original design. We were fashioned for a relationship with a good God and to walk with Him in a garden called *delight*. Yes, you read that right. He created us to live in *delight*.

> *And the LORD God planted a garden in Eden, in the east, and there he put the man whom he had formed.*
>
> —Genesis 2:8 ESV

The Hebrew word *Eden* means "pleasure or delight." Although the world we now inhabit is one marked by heartache and suffering—that was not our original state. God created us to flourish in His bountiful goodness. Sadly, we aren't in Eden anymore.

We were fashioned for life *with* God. It goes without saying that we are far from home. As we will discover, something devastating occurred in Eden—paradise was lost. The human soul was fractured in a sliver of a second as sin entered the world, disturbing the blissful union between us and Elohim. As Saint Augustine says in the *Confessions*, "Because you have made us for yourself, and our hearts find no peace until they rest in you."[1]

The human condition is *restless*. What a perfect word to describe the frantic search for meaning, the longing for more, the quest to fill the void. But in reality, we are wired for *shalom*—the peace, joy, and beauty of abiding with the God of the garden.

As we journey through the Bible, we will see the lengths to which the Lord went to bring us back into His presence, to a garden of ultimate delight. That's the message we will behold from garden to garden—how the Lord redeems, reconciles, and restores a broken humanity and makes us whole.

C. S. Lewis advises,

> If we find ourselves with a desire that nothing in this world can satisfy, the most probable explanation is that we were made for another world.[2]

## HARVEST

Do you find yourself restless or weary, longing for peace, wholeness, and joy? In what ways do you long for Eden? Take some time to sit with the Lord, with Elohim, your Creator. As we read in Psalm 16, in His Presence there is fullness of joy. As we encounter the Lord, He offers the gift of shalom. What steps can you take to carve out time to be in God's Presence each day?

1 Augustine, *Confessions* (United Kingdom: Penguin, 2004), 5.

2 C. S. Lewis, *Mere Christianity* (New York: HarperCollins, 2009), 120.

## DAY 2

# THE IMAGE-BEARERS

### SEED

*Then God said, "Let us make man in our image, after our likeness. And let them have dominion over the fish of the sea and over the birds of the heavens and over the livestock and over all the earth and over every creeping thing that creeps on the earth." So God created man in his own image, in the image of God he created him; male and female he created them.*

—Genesis 1:26–27 ESV

### CULTIVATE

Read Genesis 1; Psalm 8.

### FLOURISH

*Who are you? Why do you exist? What gives your life purpose?* These questions represent what philosophers call the human existential quest for meaning. Without a clear sense of purpose, our days feel empty and pointless. The search for significance fuels many and frustrates others because we weren't wired for an aimless existence. Discovering the reason you were created is an absolute game changer for the soul and can infuse the most mundane tasks with joy and your unseen moments with glory.

I'll never forget leading a prayer time at a women's retreat when I was surprised to discover a deep-rooted lie about life that holds many women captive. The focus of the weekend was experiencing freedom from the lies we believe about ourselves so we could walk in God's truth. As I prayed, I felt led to ask this question: "Who believes your life is meaningless?" To my surprise, hands shot up across the room. More than half of the women confessed to believing this lie.

Where does one turn to discover life's meaning? What holds the authority to define our purpose and reason for existence? As Pastor Rick Warren has said, "You didn't create yourself, so there is no way you can tell yourself what you were created for!"[1] The Bible has been coined God's Owner's Manual for Life.[2] I like that description. After all, if something malfunctioned in my car, I would check the owner's manual. The same holds true for life. To discover who I am, why I am here, and what my purpose is, then, I need to go to the "Owner's Manual."

In the opening pages of the Bible, we discover the fundamental truth about human life: We are created by God and for God. Not only are we wired for connection, but in designing us, He declared our unique purpose. We are fashioned with a soul that is meant to connect with our Creator. As profound as it seems, we are made for friendship with God.

Yesterday, we discussed Elohim, who is the Author of Life. Genesis 1:31 says, "God saw everything that he had made, and behold, it was very good" (ESV). After designing stars, light, land, fish, and birds, God did something unique. Instead of speaking,

---

1 Rick Warren, *The Purpose Driven Life: What on Earth Am I Here For?* (Grand Rapids, MI: Zondervan, 2017), 22.

2 Rick Warren, "The Bible: God's Owner's Manual for Life," April 24, 2020, PastorRick.com, https://pastorrick.com/the-bible-gods-owners-manual-for-life/.

He used His hands. The Lord stooped down to the dirt and formed a man from the dust. Then, wonder of wonders, God breathed His own breath into him, "and the man became a living creature" (Gen. 2:7 ESV).

Imagine this moment. First, Adam's lifeless form was molded by Elohim's hands. Then, God exhaled, and His breath entered Adam's lungs! In the next scene, God fashioned Eve, the first woman, and together they are given this extraordinary title—image-bearers of God.

So far, humanity is off to a stellar start. God didn't give giraffes or golden retrievers His breath; that distinction is placed on humans. It is the breath of God that separates us from all other created beings.

Additionally, we are also endowed with God-given dignity—we are made in His image. In Latin, this is called the *Imago Dei*. According to our SEED focal passage, every human bears this divine stamp. But what does it mean to bear His image? We can look up at the night sky and see our purpose. Just as the moon reflects the light of the sun, so we were designed to reflect God's glory to the world.

Radiant with the light of God, our purpose is to emanate His beauty, truth, and goodness. Each individual human is created with unique gifts, talents, and abilities to reflect the wisdom and beauty of Elohim to the world.

Next, our "Owner's Manual" tells us that God gave His image-bearers dominion to rule over His creation. *Dominion* is not a word we use every day, but I would suggest that it is the very truth that gives ultimate meaning to our daily living. *Dominion* means "to rule or reign." God made us kings and queens, with delegated authority over all He made. Just as Adam and Eve were tasked with cultivating and keeping the Garden of Eden, so we are called to cause the world around us to flourish. As we tend and keep the families, communities, and countries in which God places us, His glory shines forth. Understanding this calling gives significance to the ordinary tasks of life. When we cultivate a home, build a business, or lead in government, we exercise our God-given dominion and reflect His glory to the world.

Finally, the Bible also teaches that we were made in God's likeness. This doesn't mean we are gods, but rather that we are like Him mentally, morally, and socially. We are like God in that we have free will and moral conscience, and we are relational beings. These are deep theological waters, but the seed of truth I pray blooms in your heart is that your life is not meaningless! You are an image-bearer of God whose life holds great purpose, dignity, and value. As Randy Alcorn rightly states, "Mankind was designed to live on the earth to God's glory."[3]

While the Bible explains our original design, we all look in the mirror and face a broken image-bearer. We don't reflect God's glory as intended. Our world isn't flourishing but fractured. What went wrong? As we will see tomorrow, something happened in Eden that marred the image of God in all of us: Sin entered the human heart.

Although God's image is distorted, all is not lost. God is in the restoration business. He takes the broken and makes something beautiful. Our lives still hold incomparable glory. And if we place them in the hands of our Maker, we discover the reason we have breath in our bones. The One who fashioned us with such magnificent design is the One who can redeem, restore, and use our lives for a glorious purpose!

*For by him all things were created, in heaven and on earth, visible and invisible, whether thrones or dominions or rulers*

---

3 Randy Alcorn, *Heaven* (Carol Stream, IL: Tyndale House, 2011), 92.

*or authorities—all things were created through him and for him.*

—Colossians 1:16 ESV

## HARVEST

Do you believe your life has significant purpose because you are an image-bearer of God? Or have you also believed the lie that your life is meaningless? Take a moment to reflect on the truth that you were created uniquely to reflect God's image and glory to the world. What are some ways you can begin to live for His glory today?

DAY 3

# THE SERPENT

## SEED

*Now the serpent was more crafty than any other beast of the field that the LORD God had made. He said to the woman, "Did God actually say, 'You shall not eat of any tree in the garden'?"*

—Genesis 3:1–2 ESV

## CULTIVATE

Read Genesis 3:1–7; Romans 1; Ephesians 6:10–12.

## FLOURISH

We all long for Eden. Whenever we hear of a terminal diagnosis, watch a child suffer, learn of an injustice, or wrestle with our own dark thoughts, we instinctively know that this world is broken. What happened to us?

As we've seen in God's Word, Adam and Eve dwelled in paradise with God. Their reality was so far from our reality that it is hard to even imagine. The biblical language tells us that Eden was a fertile and fruitful abode. I like to imagine Hawaii without a hint of humidity or an ounce of perspiration. The Garden of Eden was a place marked by God's provision, presence, and loving protection. It was God's great love for His image-bearers that not only provided for all their needs but also warned them of a great danger:

> *You may surely eat of every tree of the garden, but of the tree of the knowledge of good and evil you shall not eat, for in the day that you eat of it you shall surely die.*
>
> —Genesis 2:16–17 ESV

Like a good Father who desires to protect His child, the Lord gave a command to which all parents can relate. Even though a toddler may not understand why the stove is off-limits, the parent knows. The same proves true in this scenario. God knew why "the tree of the knowledge of good and evil" was harmful for the human race; therefore, He issued a rule to protect them. Adam and Eve were called to trust God's goodness and believe that His command was intended to bless them.

Into the bliss and bounty of Eden slithered a Serpent. We know from God's Word that this Serpent is Satan, God's Enemy who seeks to kill, steal, and destroy God's image-bearers (see John 10:10). The snake confronted Eve with a question: "Did God actually say, 'You shall not eat of any tree in the garden'?" (Gen. 3:1 ESV). First of all, we discover that Satan's first weapon is doubt. He knows if we doubt God's Word then he can lead us into temptation, which leads to his ultimate goal—our destruction.

Eve responded by saying they were permitted to eat from all the trees of the garden—except one. This tree was prohibited because the eating of it would bring death. The Serpent then hissed out his poisonous accusation: "You will not surely die. For God knows that when you eat of it your eyes will be opened, and you will be like God, knowing good and evil" (Gen. 3:4–5 ESV).

Let's take a closer look at the Serpent's MO (modus operandi; mode of operation). First, Satan caused Eve to doubt God's word. Then he made an accusation against God's character by implying that God was withholding something good. Then, the Serpent tempted Eve to ignore God's command and take for herself the forbidden fruit by offering various reasons to justify her rebellion.

Eve responded to the tempter with a two-step dance called rationalization and justification. She rationalized that the fruit seemed good for food and justified that it was desirable for gaining wisdom, but most alluring of all was that they would be "like God."

No longer content to just be His image-bearers, Eve reasoned that by taking the fruit they could choose for themselves, call the shots, and be their own god! The lure to live for self rather than for the glory of God proved the strongest temptation. With a shrug she surmised, "What's the worst that could happen?" Oh, Eve, the worst did happen! And with the juice running down her face, she handed a piece to Adam, and he ate.

One bite brought sin and death crashing into the garden. The seed of this cosmic rebellion has borne fruit for every generation. Hatred, abuse, addictions, lies, injustice, greed, insecurity, murder, pride, lust, envy, and disease are just a few of the poisonous fruits growing from this rebellious bite.

In the coming days, we will examine the fallout of this catastrophic choice when Adam and Eve believed Satan's lies rather than believing God's truth. The human experience would now be marked by shame, emptiness, suffering, and longing for our true home. Now those of us made as God's image-bearers would struggle with disordered desires. Instead of loving and exalting our Creator, we would love and exalt created things. This reversal brought bondage to the human soul as we became enslaved to anything we elevated to godlike status in our lives.

Randy Alcorn states,

> Sin and death and suffering and war and poverty are not natural—they are the devastating results of our rebellion

> against God. We long for a return to Paradise—a perfect world, without the corruption of sin, where God walks with us and talks with us in the cool of the day.[1]

It's plain to see that Satan lied to Eve, saying, "You will not surely die!" While the Lord graciously didn't strike Adam and Eve dead on the spot, the moment they ate the forbidden fruit, they did experience spiritual death (separation from God). Then, the process of physical death began to set in. As a result of the original sin, all humanity is now separated from God and under the curse of death. In addition to being born in sin, we've all listened to the Serpent's lies, rebelled from our Creator, and attempted to live for our own glory.

Since the dawn of time, a battle has raged over the coveted spot of center stage; this is the war for glory. This cosmic conflict is fought by Satan, God's adversary and the Enemy of humanity, and the Creator Himself. The Bible teaches us that Satan was originally the most beautiful of God's creatures in heaven. He was the chief angel, whose specific purpose was to reflect the light of God's glory, but evil entered his heart and he craved this brilliance for himself. Because of his desire to be the famous one, Satan (at that time called Lucifer, the morning star) was cast out of heaven, taking one-third of the angelic host with him (see Rev. 12:1–12; Ezek. 28:11–19; Isa. 14:12–17).

This is where you and I enter the scene. When God created the world, He established it in perfection. He placed Adam and Eve in the Garden of Eden and gave them dominion and purpose (see Gen. 1–2). It was there that Satan attacked God's glory by tempting Eve into sin (see Gen. 3:1–4). He deceived her into believing happiness could be found by seeking her own glory,

---

1 Alcorn, *Heaven*, 78.

instead of the glory of her Creator. He promised her power, prestige, and position—to be somebody who is made much of (see Gen. 3:5). Eve took the bait and so did Adam, resulting in all of humanity falling from glory.

Today, we battle the same Enemy and face the same choice in every temptation—glorify self or glorify God? All sin comes down to this one question. In seeking our own glory, we find emptiness, destruction, and death simply because we are choosing to turn the purpose of life upside down.

Jesus taught that sin isn't just something we have (like a cold virus); sin is something that has us. It is something that holds us in captivity, refusing to let us go. We don't have control over it; it has control over us. The picture is a slave controlled by a master. Sin holds us captive and refuses to let us go unless a ransom is paid, which is precisely what God did to solve our problem.

> *Truly, truly, I say to you, everyone who practices sin is a slave to sin. The slave does not remain in the house forever; the son remains forever. So if the Son sets you free, you will be free indeed.*
>
> —John 8:34–36 ESV

Today we learned of the bad news of what happened to humanity. Sin is not just something we do; it is now part of our operating system. Humans have proved terrible at being our own god. Thankfully, the story doesn't end with Adam and Eve wiping the fruit from their lips. The Bible reveals God's amazing grace and declares that redemption is His specialty.

Randy Alcorn tells us,

> While the wound of sin was still fresh, before the first scar had formed, God unveiled his plan to send a fully human

> redeemer who would be far more powerful than Satan. In a courageous act of intervention to deliver mankind, this redeemer would deliver a mortal wound to the usurping devil, and in the process would be wounded himself.[2]

The Lord made a way to bring us back home. Just as the fall came through the eating of the forbidden tree, so redemption would come through a tree—the old rugged cross where Jesus Christ was crucified. On that tree, Jesus took on the sin and shame of the world so that we could take on forgiveness, life, and freedom. We call this the Good News. Although today we looked at the bad news of the human story, the greatest news of all—the Gospel—is that anyone who hopes in Jesus is saved from sin and can be reconciled with God.

> *For the wages of sin is death, but the free gift of God is eternal life in Christ Jesus our Lord.*
>
> —Romans 6:23 ESV

## HARVEST

Most temptation begins with doubt. Just as Satan did with Eve in the garden, our adversary plants seeds of doubt in our minds about the goodness of God and the truthfulness of His Word. Take a minute to think through the ways you are tempted to disobey God or turn from His purpose for your life. How has doubt played a role in your struggle? As you sit with the Lord, confess your questions and fears to God. Ask Him to give you faith to believe and a mind renewed by His truth.

---

2 Alcorn, *Heaven*, 99.

## DAY 4

# THE WEEDS OF SIN

### SEED

*Then the eyes of both were opened, and they knew that they were naked. And they sewed fig leaves together and made themselves loincloths. And they heard the sound of the LORD God walking in the garden in the cool of the day, and the man and his wife hid themselves from the presence of the LORD God among the trees of the garden.*

—Genesis 3:7–8 ESV

### CULTIVATE

Read Genesis 3:7–19; Romans 3:11–26; 10:11.

### FLOURISH

I was enjoying a meal with some friends when one woman began lamenting issues in her life. She confessed to struggling with anger and addiction. She shared her insecurities and fears, then casually added, "But it's not my fault. I'm this way because of my dad." While I applaud her transparency and empathize with her struggles, what concerned me was how quickly she played the blame game.

We all have generational baggage, but we can't experience freedom until we own it and bring it to God for forgiveness and healing. I knew my friend was open to hearing the truth, so I lovingly cautioned her about playing the blame game. I said, "I get it. I experienced childhood trauma, too. I have my own issues. But we can point the finger for our problems all the way back to the Garden of Eden. Sure, our parents sinned against us, but so did their parents before them, and on it goes. We can place blame back through every generation until we finally arrive at Adam and Eve."

In this fallen world, we are sinned against. Wrong has been done to us, and that trauma has left its mark. But we are also born with a sinful nature—we have our own selfishness, pride, vanity, prejudices, and ways we've hurt others. Sin is a reality in our post-Eden world. Instead of a garden paradise, we live in a world filled with thorns and thistles. After Adam and Eve tasted the forbidden fruit, the weeds of fear, guilt, shame, and blame sprouted in the soil of the human heart.

Weeds in a garden compete with other plants for resources like water, nutrients, sunshine, and space. In the garden of our soul, the weeds that sprouted after the fall compete for the love, joy, freedom, and life that God intended for us to have as His image-bearers.

One of the first weeds that sprouted in the human heart was separation from God. Remember, Adam and Eve enjoyed perfect friendship with the Lord. But when they rebelled, that fellowship was broken. They became aware of their guilt and were ashamed before Him. As a result, they hid from God's Presence (see Gen. 3:8–10), and, sadly, we've been hiding ever since.

Fear causes us to run from God rather than run to Him. Although God is our Creator and loving Heavenly Father, sin in all of us runs in fear from His Presence. Some hide by pushing the very thought of God out of their minds; others hide by believing lies about His character and running away. Hiding takes many forms, but the root of this weed goes back to original sin.

The second weed that sprouted in the human soul after sin was shame. Scripture gives us an insightful commentary about Adam and Eve's state before the fall: "They were not ashamed" (Gen. 2:25 ESV). The weed of shame sprouted quickly and has dominated the landscape of humanity ever since.

Sometimes people confuse guilt and shame, and it's important that we distinguish between the two. Guilt is the knowledge that says, "I did wrong." Shame, on the other hand, is the feeling that says, "I am wrong." While guilt deals with our behavior, shame on the other hand focuses on our identity. Shame is the voice that says because of what you've done, "You are unlovable. Your sin is unforgivable. You are dirty. You are wretched." Shame is the voice of the Enemy, who wants to keep us trapped in our sin.

Instinctively, Adam and Eve knew something was dreadfully wrong after they rebelled against the Lord. That was guilt, which led to their hiding. But what they did next was evidence of the shameful voice whispering in their ears. Adam and Eve made garments of fig leaves to cover themselves. Although their solution was inadequate, they desperately attempted to cover their shame.

Friends, we are far from the Garden of Eden, but we still wear fig leaves. Any time we try to hide our imperfections and grasp for love, we are using fig leaves to cover shame. We try to overcome the voice that says we are unlovable, unforgivable, or unwanted. We grasp at a variety of ways to try to earn acceptance. What does this look like? Some examples include a lack of transparency with others, people-pleasing, religious activity, perfectionism, a chronic need for approval, and much of our addictive behavior.

God is so good. Genesis 3:9 tells us the Lord pursued Adam and Eve in their hiding. Although they had rebelled, He came looking for them to reveal His plan of redemption. Giving us a glimpse of God's grace, we see the Lord pursue them—not to punish, but to free them from the weeds!

When the Lord called out to them, He asked several questions: Where are you? Who told you? What did you do? God's questions prompted them to admit the problem so He could bring the right solution for their sin and shame.

Finally, we see one more weed in the garden—blame. When the Lord asked the questions, they responded by pointing the finger. Adam blamed Eve, Eve blamed the Serpent, and that snake... well, that story is for another day. Sin not only fractured the human soul but also our relationships with one another. What was once marked by intimacy with God and each other is now characterized by finger-pointing and faultfinding.

The Lord brought Adam and Eve out of their hiding spot and removed their fig leaves. God took an animal, killed it, and used the skin of the animal to cover their nakedness. This was the first death recorded in the Bible, and it occurred in the Garden of Eden to deal with the problem of shame.

Sin has consequences. We are separated from God. We live in fear and hiding. And we constantly battle the voice of shame. But thankfully, the Bible doesn't end in Genesis 3, and we don't have to live forever strangled by these weeds. Romans 8:1–2 tells us, "There is therefore now no condemnation for those who are in Christ Jesus. For the law of the Spirit of life has set you free in Christ Jesus from the law of sin and death" (ESV). No condemnation means "no more shame!" Why? Jesus took the guilt of our sin and shame on the cross so that we can take on His perfect righteousness and freedom. When we look to Christ as our covering, we can come out of hiding, where we are enveloped by grace and experience true freedom from the voice of shame!

*I sought the LORD, and he answered me*
*and delivered me from all my fears.*
*Those who look to him are radiant,*
*and their faces shall never be ashamed.*

—Psalm 34:4–5 ESV

## HARVEST

Are you struggling under the weight of shame? Spend some time asking the Lord to take away your shame—He does not want you covered in it! Reread Romans 8:1–2 and Psalm 34:4–5 above, and with intent, name the fig leaves you are using to cover any shame. Release them and ask the Lord to cover you with His grace. He delights in lavishing it upon you!

— DAY 5 —

# THE SEED OF THE WOMAN

## SEED

*So the LORD God said to the serpent: "Because you have done this, you are cursed more than all cattle, and more than every beast of the field; on your belly you shall go, and you shall eat dust all the days of your life. And I will put enmity between you and the woman, and between your seed and her Seed; He shall bruise your head, and you shall bruise His heel."*

—Genesis 3:14–15 NKJV

## CULTIVATE

Read Genesis 3:14–24; Romans 5; 8:1–2.

## FLOURISH

I love a movie with a great plot twist—a surprise turn of events I didn't see coming. There are many contenders, but the moment in *The Empire Strikes Back* when Darth Vader says to Luke Skywalker, "I am your father," goes down in history as one of the biggest movie surprises of all time.

Move over, *Star Wars*—the Bible reveals the ultimate plot twist. In Genesis 3:1–9, we left Adam and Eve in the Garden of Eden experiencing the guilt and shame of their terrible choice.

What one would expect from such a cosmic rebellion is God storming into Eden with guns blazing and bringing total retaliation upon the guilty sinners.

Plot twist! That's not what happened! Instead of revenge, we see the Lord graciously seeking out the guilty, confronting their sin, promising restoration, and covering their shame. We see a God who pursues the sinner and offers hope for the future.

As the Bible proceeds from garden to garden, it includes four major divisions: Creation, Fall, Redemption, and Restoration. Throughout this grand narrative, we behold the character of God and discover He is a God of amazing grace who wrote a love story that played out on the pages of human history. We also learn a great deal about ourselves as we see a reflection of our humanity in the men and women whose lives are part of this great redemption story.

Today's SEED passage proves to be one of the most important in the Bible, which is an understatement of magnificent proportions! Genesis 3 sets the stage for everything we read in the rest of the Scripture as the entire human saga points back to Adam and Eve's fatal choice and the fallout that occurred.

The story of the fall answers many questions:

What happened to us?

Why are we searching for meaning and fulfillment?

Why are relationships so complicated?

Why are we prone to selfishness, violence, greed, lust, and corruption?

Diving into this passage, we learn much about the Lord: He is a God of justice. Sin indeed has consequences for humanity and creation. No longer would work be a joy, but now a constant struggle. Thorns and thistles would become the norm. (I'd like to add mosquitoes, humidity, and traffic to that list, but I digress!)

Childbearing would be painful. (Ladies, we will have a chat with Eve about this one.) And a continual power struggle would mark male-and-female relationships.

But in the midst of explaining the natural consequences of their rebellion, God revealed that He is the Redeemer by promising ultimate victory over the Serpent and the sin he introduced into the world. This promise holds the key to unlocking the entire Bible. The Lord said to the serpent: "I will put enmity between you and the woman, and between your seed and her Seed; He shall bruise your head, and you shall bruise His heel" (Gen. 3:15 NKJV).

From this curse upon the Serpent shines forth the most incredible beacon of hope the fallen world has ever known. God promised a Seed, or the offspring of a woman, who would come to crush the head of the Serpent. As the Bible progresses, the identity of the "Seed of the woman" becomes clearer.

Spoiler alert! That promised "Seed" is Jesus Christ. Born of a woman, fully God and fully man, He came to crush the head of the Serpent! As the Nicene Creed describes Jesus, "For us and for our salvation he came down from heaven; he became incarnate by the Holy Spirit and the virgin Mary, and was made human."[1] The prophecy of the Seed of the woman crushing the Serpent's head points forward thousands of years to Jesus' death on the cross that defeated Satan and fully accomplished the salvation of all who would trust Him as Savior.

We will discover many more prophecies concerning Jesus in the Bible. But in Genesis 3:15, the Lord predicted the ultimate showdown between Satan and Jesus. Satan would "bruise His heel" (NKJV) at the cross, a prophecy fulfilled when the nails were driven through Jesus' feet. But Jesus would crush the Serpent's head by rising from the dead and bringing ultimate victory over

---

1 Andrew E. Burn, *The Nicene Creed* (London: Rivingtons, 1909).

Satan, sin, and death. As 1 John 3:8 says, "The reason the Son of God appeared was to destroy the works of the devil" (ESV).

Although the Lord promised a future hope for humanity, He still showed mercy to Adam and Eve by expelling them from the garden. As Genesis 3:24 says, "He drove out the man, and at the east of the garden of Eden he placed the cherubim and a flaming sword that turned every way to guard the way to the tree of life" (ESV).

The Tree of Life is one of the most significant symbols in the entire Bible and bookends the beginning and end of Scripture. In Genesis, the Tree of Life appears to have been a source of eternal life. Adam and Eve were designed to live forever, but to do so they likely needed to eat from the Tree of Life. Once they sinned, because of their eating of the forbidden tree, they were banned from the garden and subject to physical death, just as they had experienced spiritual death. Since Eden, the curse of death has reigned. It was an act of tremendous mercy that moved God to protect Adam and Eve from eating of the Tree of Life in their sinful state.

How was exile from Eden merciful? Our gracious God knew the eternal agony of sin was too much for humanity to bear; therefore, He stationed a mighty angelic being to block their path. Adam and Eve's last glimpse of Eden was the flaming sword guarding the way back into the Garden of Eden.

Paradise was lost. What a tragic scene, but thankfully we know the rest of the story. Although Genesis 3 tells the origin of sin and the fall of humanity, it truly offers us a glimpse of God's amazing grace. Here we are introduced to the Lord, who doesn't give us what we deserve but instead He pursues us, protects us, and offers us the hope of redemption.

*Redemption.* This word spills over the brim with promise. Before we see the fruition of that promise, we will first enter the "Exile" portion of the biblical story. For the next ten days we will dive into God's Word and see what happened when Adam and Eve left Eden. As we trace the consequences of sin and the fall in the human story, we will see how God called out one man to be the father of faith through which the Savior of the world would come. Day by day through the exile from Eden, we will wait with expectation for God's divine plan of redemption to unfold, which brings the exiled soul back home to God the Father.

> *But when the fullness of time had come, God sent forth his Son, born of woman, born under the law, to redeem those who were under the law, so that we might receive adoption as sons. And because you are sons, God has sent the Spirit of his Son into our hearts, crying, "Abba! Father!"*
>
> —Galatians 4:4–6 ESV

## HARVEST

You don't have to look far to see the evidence of the fall. In fact, we all experience its repercussions every day. How does it impact the way you view the world's brokenness and suffering to know that God sent His Son, Jesus, to redeem this fallen world and that you are included in His work of restoration?

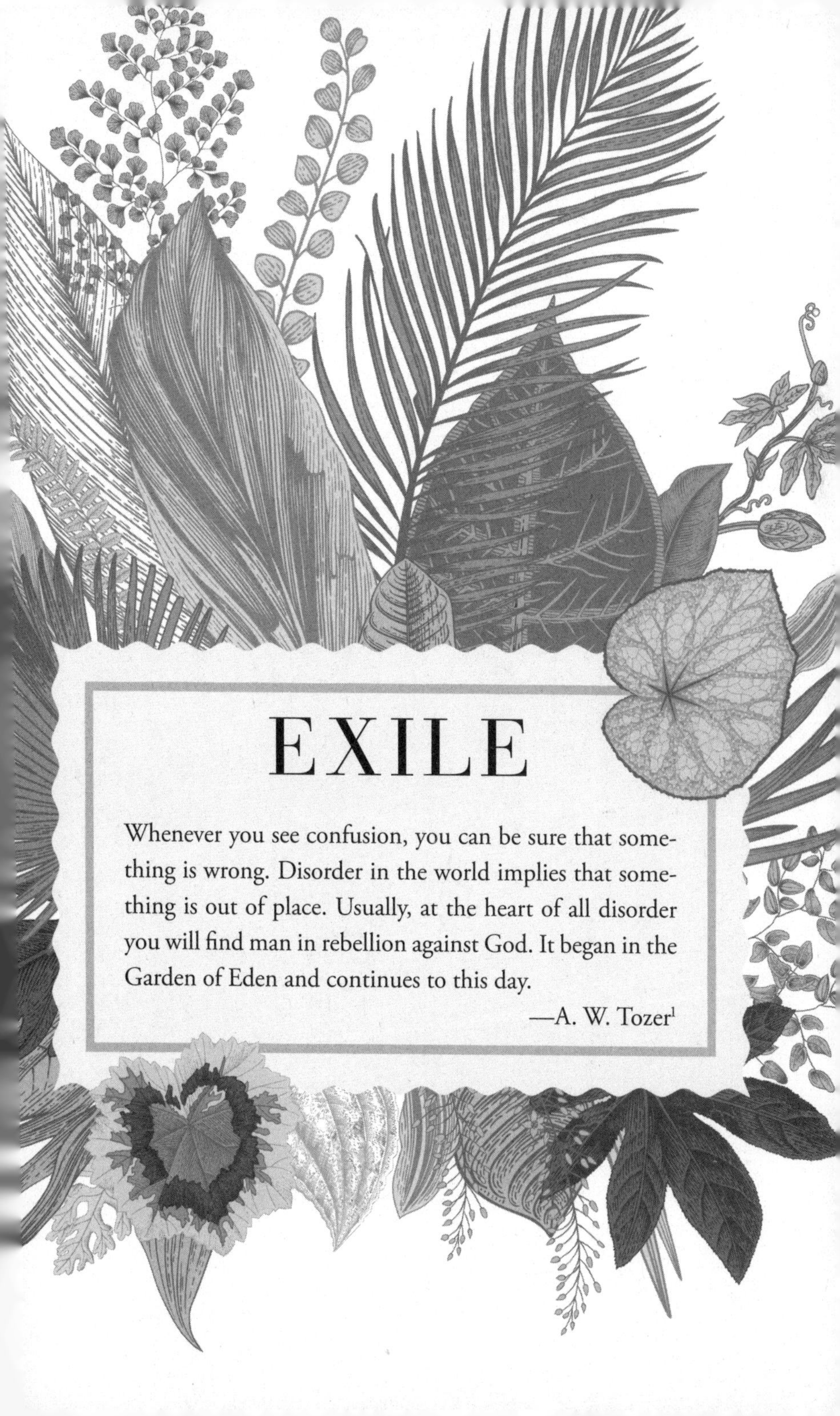

# EXILE

Whenever you see confusion, you can be sure that something is wrong. Disorder in the world implies that something is out of place. Usually, at the heart of all disorder you will find man in rebellion against God. It began in the Garden of Eden and continues to this day.

—A. W. Tozer[1]

Footnote citation from page 31:

1 A. W. Tozer, *And He Dwelt Among Us: Teachings from the Gospel of John* (Grand Rapids, MI: Baker, 2009), 47.

DAY 6

# THE BLESSING OF ABRAHAM

## SEED

*Now the LORD said to Abram, "Go from your country and your kindred and your father's house to the land that I will show you. And I will make of you a great nation, and I will bless you and make your name great, so that you will be a blessing. I will bless those who bless you, and him who dishonors you I will curse, and in you all the families of the earth shall be blessed."*

—Genesis 12:1–3 ESV

## CULTIVATE

Read Genesis 12:1–8; 17:1–19; Hebrews 11:7–12.

## FLOURISH

Although I wasn't a follower of Christ until I was twenty-five years old, I did grow up in church and was exposed to Bible teachings as a child. One of my earliest memories is from Vacation Bible School when I was about six years old. Aside from the games and snacks, I learned a song with hand motions that went a little something like this:

Father Abraham had many sons,
many sons had Father Abraham
I am one of them, and so are you,
so let's all praise the Lord![1]

Why do children across the globe sing about a nomadic man who lived thousands of years ago? It was nearly three decades and one master's degree in biblical theology later before I comprehended the meaning of that little song.

Abraham proves to be one of the most important characters in the Bible. He marks a turning point in the redemptive story, and world history hinges upon his faith. But vital to our journey from garden to garden through the Bible is understanding how Abraham links Eden and eternity. He stands as the direct connection between Adam and Eve and the "Seed of the woman" who would crush the head of the Serpent.

After Adam and Eve were exiled from Eden, Genesis traces their descendants to Noah, a man God called to build an ark because He was bringing a flood upon the earth. Genesis 6:5–6 explains the reason for the flood: "The LORD saw that the wickedness of man was great in the earth, and that every intention of the thoughts of his heart was only evil continually. And the LORD regretted that he had made man on the earth, and it grieved him to his heart" (ESV).

Evil and wickedness reigned on earth, and God chose to start anew through Noah. Although he faced public ridicule as he built a boat and warned the world of the coming flood, Noah believed God and entered the ark. Therefore, out of all the families of

---

1 H. P. Robbins and K. N. Wolf, *Make a Joyful Noise! Music, Movement, and Creative Play to Teach Bible Stories: Preschool–Grade 1* (Quezon City, Philippines: New Day, 2007), 78.

the earth, the promised "Seed of the woman" would now come through Noah's family.

After the flood, the line of descent is drawn from Noah's son Shem to Abram. While these genealogies may seem dull to read, they establish a vital connection between Adam and Abraham. The Bible wants us to know that the expected Redeemer, or "Seed of the woman," would be an offspring of this man.

According to John Piper,

> Man was made to rely on God and give him glory. Instead, man chose to rely on himself and seek his own glory—to make a name for himself. So God elected one small person and promised to achieve his purpose through that man and his descendants. He would make Abram's name great, so that he, and not man, would get the glory.[2]

Abram, whose name would be changed by God to Abraham, first appeared on the pages of Scripture at a dark point in the human story. Humanity was on a downhill spiral after the exile from Eden. The consequences of sin were human selfishness, hateful murder, pagan idolatry, and dysfunctional relationships. Paradise was lost, and it sure seemed like Satan had won. But in this dismal state, God called out one man. Smack in the middle of the exile from Eden we find God's grace. Abraham's calling is a striking picture of grace—for Abraham did nothing to merit God's choosing him out of the darkness.

In Genesis 12, the Lord appeared to Abram and told him to leave his old life and go to a land that He would show him. In our SEED focal passage (vv. 1–3), we read that the Lord promised to

---

2 John Piper, "God Created Us for His Glory," https://www.desiringgod.org/messages/god-created-us-for-his-glory.

bless Abram, to make of him a great nation, and through him bring blessing to all the nations of the earth.

These promises are called the Abrahamic covenant. A covenant is a binding agreement between two parties. In this case, the two parties are the Lord God Almighty and Abraham. Essentially, God said, "I will be your God and you will be My people."

Abraham responded to the divine invitation to "go" with an obedient and hearty "yes." Without knowing how God would fulfill the promise, Father Abraham put his yes on the table and went all in with the Lord. Genesis tells us that he set out for the land of Canaan. He simply believed the promise and trusted the Lord to work out the details. Although the years were not easy and his faith was tested on many occasions, Abraham believed God.

His biggest test of faith was due to the fact that Abraham's wife, Sarah, was barren. For years they hoped for a child and waited on the Lord for the fulfillment of the word. But as the decades crept by, so did their hope of conceiving a child in the natural way. During their waiting, the Lord took him outside and said, "'Look now toward heaven, and count the stars if you are able to number them.' And He said to him, 'So shall your descendants be'" (Gen. 15:5 NKJV). God promised Abraham something that was impossible in the natural realm—offspring as numerous as the stars! And Scripture records this incredible truth:

> *And he believed the LORD, and he counted it to him as righteousness.*
>
> —Genesis 15:6 ESV

Abraham's part in the miracle was to believe God. Faith was the only thing Abraham brought to the table of grace. Unlike Adam and Eve, who didn't believe God and listened to the Serpent, Abraham believed the Lord. Righteousness means to have a right standing with God. Even though he lived in a depraved world broken by sin, Abraham was right with God because of his faith. And as a result, he was called a friend of God (see James 2:23).

As Scripture unfolds, we see how God fulfilled His promises to Abraham. First, the Lord miraculously opened Sarah's womb and provided them with a child. That son, Isaac, would be the carrier of the covenant blessing and next in the prophetic line from Adam to the promised Redeemer.

Abraham's life was marked with twists and turns, yet throughout his story, we see God's hand at work to bring about His promises. The way back into God's Presence would go directly through a descendant of Abraham, Jesus Christ—the One through whom God would indeed bless the whole world.

God chose Abraham out of all the people of the earth to bring about the family through whom the fellowship lost in Eden would be redeemed. Through this man, who was called a friend of God, our own friendship with God can be restored.

*And if you are Christ's, then you are Abraham's offspring,*
*heirs according to promise.*

—Galatians 3:29 ESV

## HARVEST

Is friendship with God something you're familiar with, or does that seem like a strange concept? As we read today, Abraham, the great father of faith, was called a friend of God. But friendship with God isn't granted only to the heroes of the Bible. Jesus calls those of us who follow Him friends, too! (See John 15:14–15.) Let that sink in—the Almighty God desires a relationship with you, and He calls you friend! How does this truth impact the way you approach Him?

## DAY 7

# THE LORD WILL PROVIDE

### SEED

*So Abraham called the name of that place, "The LORD will provide"; as it is said to this day, "On the mount of the LORD it shall be provided."*

—Genesis 22:14 ESV

### CULTIVATE

Read Genesis 22:1–18; Hebrews 11:1–19.

### FLOURISH

Waiting on God proves to be one of the most painful seasons many of us will ever face. Living with an unmet desire is a crucible. Whether you're waiting for healing or have spent years hoping for a spouse, you know the ache I'm talking about. Anyone struggling with infertility knows the longing for a child. And those in a financial crisis understand the mounting pressure of needing a breakthrough. In the fire of delayed answers, what we believe about the Lord (His character, power, and purposes for us) is tested. The soil of unmet desires is fertile ground for bitterness, but it is also where miracles happen.

Abraham understood this crucible better than most. He was seventy-five years old when the Lord established the covenant with him. The covenant included the Promised Land, descendants as numerous as the stars, and a future blessing for the entire world. Abraham left everything to follow the Lord. Then he waited. He was one hundred years old (and his wife was ninety) when their son, Isaac, was finally born. Altogether, they waited twenty-five years for their miracle child.

In those years, they begged for confirmation, battled doubt, and tried to help God out. They attempted to bring about the promise through a surrogate woman named Hagar. But a human solution was not how God planned to bring about His promised offspring.

In His perfect timing, the Lord supernaturally enabled Sarah to conceive, and Isaac was born. His name means "laughter"—which was fitting, since he brought joy to his parents and a few chuckles to their friends.

But after Abraham's family settled into their blessing, God tested him. Genesis 22 shares the details of this test—when the Lord asked Abraham to sacrifice Isaac. These words prove hard for anyone to read—trust me, as a mother, they are painful to even write.

Why this test? First, God is not sadistic and does not delight in suffering. Second, from Scripture, we know the Lord hates human sacrifice. So, we can safely assume God had a different purpose in this test. One reason was to test Abraham's loyalty. Did he love the gift more than the Giver? But I believe the primary reason was to foreshadow the worldwide blessing the Lord promised to bring through Abraham's seed and to demonstrate to this man of faith the great price of this redemption.

The Lord said, "Take your son, your only son Isaac, whom you love, and go to the land of Moriah, and offer him there as a burnt offering on one of the mountains of which I shall tell you" (Gen.

22:2 ESV). Abraham obeyed *immediately*. The very next morning, Abraham saddled his donkey and headed for the land the Lord would show him.

It was a three-day journey to the region of Moriah. This was quite a trek for an old man! With each step, he had to ponder the divine instructions and walk by faith in his God. Finally, they arrived at the land of Moriah, where Abraham built an altar for the Lord.

A few observations about Isaac are in order. First, the Lord called him "The son whom you love." It's worth noting that this is the very first mention of the word *love* in the Bible. Second, notice that he carried the instruments for his death, the fire and wood, as he followed his father up Mount Moriah. Isaac was old enough to understand a sacrifice was being prepared and he carried the instruments for it. But then he asked an important question: "Where is the lamb for a burnt offering?" (Gen. 22:7 ESV).

Abraham offered a prophetic answer to his child: "God will provide for himself the lamb for a burnt offering" (Gen. 22:8 ESV). The man of faith believed God would provide. He knew the covenant promises were tied to this young man's destiny. Therefore, Abraham reasoned that God would somehow intervene. As Hebrews 11:19 tells us, "He considered that God was able even to raise him from the dead" (ESV).

Despite not knowing *how* God would intervene, Abraham obeyed. He took the knife, and as he prepared to plunge it into his son, he heard a voice cry out:

> *Do not lay your hand on the boy or do anything to him, for now I know that you fear God, seeing you have not withheld your son, your only son, from me.*
>
> —Genesis 22:12 ESV

I have goose bumps as I contemplate the next scene. Abraham lifted his eyes from his son's and saw a ram providentially caught in the thicket. As expected, the Lord provided!

> *And Abraham lifted up his eyes and looked, and behold, behind him was a ram, caught in a thicket by his horns. And Abraham went and took the ram and offered it up as a burnt offering instead of his son.*
>
> —Genesis 22:13 ESV

Just as Abraham believed, the Lord provided the lamb! The ram died in place of Isaac. In a beautiful turn of events, a substitute became the sacrifice. This act laid the groundwork for the sacrificial system in the Old Testament. This divine intervention also pointed forward to Jesus, who would die in the place of all who put their hope in Him for salvation. Theologians call this substitutionary atonement, which is a million-dollar phrase that means a sacrifice dies in the place of a sinner and the death of the sacrifice pays for the sin of the offeror.

Friends, God is in the details. Mount Moriah is where the city of Jerusalem would be established—the exact spot where King Solomon would build the Temple (see 2 Chron. 3:1). There, every day in the Temple in Jerusalem, lambs were offered to God to die in the place of sinners—just as the ram died in the place of Isaac. But most importantly, on Mount Moriah in Jerusalem is where God offered His Son, Jesus Christ, to die in the place of me and you.

On Mount Moriah is a ragged rock called Golgotha (see John 19:17–18). And just like Isaac before Him, Jesus trekked to the top of that hill, carrying the very instrument of His own death—an old rugged cross. But this time, there was no ram caught in the thicket to spare Him. Jesus was the Lamb of God. Abraham said that the Lord would provide the lamb, and He did. At the top of Mount Moriah, Jesus was crucified. Jesus came for this very purpose—to die in our place so that we can be reconciled to God.

> *For God so loved the world, that he gave his only Son, that whoever believes in him should not perish but have eternal life.*
>
> —John 3:16 ESV

## HARVEST

God provided a substitute in what had to be one of the most harrowing moments of Abraham's life. Our SEED verse today tells us that afterward, Abraham called the place "The LORD will provide" (Gen. 22:14). The Hebrew word for "provide" is *Jireh*, and this is where we see God's name as Jehovah Jireh—*the LORD will provide.* Is there a situation in your life for which you need God's provision? Can you relate to the agony Abraham must have felt as he awaited the provision? Friend, you can call on Jehovah Jireh in your time of need and trust that He will provide His best for you.

— DAY 8 —

# THE PROVIDENCE OF GOD

## SEED

*But Joseph said to them, "Do not fear, for am I in the place of God? As for you, you meant evil against me, but God meant it for good, to bring it about that many people should be kept alive, as they are today."*

—Genesis 50:19–20 ESV

## CULTIVATE

Read Genesis 37; 50:15–21.

## FLOURISH

I love a good comeback story. You know the kind—when the hero is knocked down, but not knocked out. From the ashes they rise, wipe the dust off, and finish what they started. The Bible is filled with such comebacks—the ultimate one being Jesus Christ's comeback, of course. With resurrection on His résumé, He's the Comeback King! However, others in the biblical narrative also seemed utterly defeated; yet they emerged victorious. Chief among them is a man named Joseph.

Joseph's life, marked by rejection, suffering, and false accusations, has proved to be a healing balm to my soul. In my own seasons of darkness, God used this man's life to illustrate how He can work all things, including injustice and heartbreak, for our good and His glory. Joseph's journey teaches us that our darkest days are not our destiny. When in the grip of defeat, we are comforted knowing God is not finished and specializes in taking what the Enemy meant for evil and working it for our good.

Joseph plays a significant role in the grand narrative of redemption. His life is like a tapestry, a beautiful work of art composed of threads of yarn, dark and light, woven together to create a masterpiece. What's striking is that if we focus on just one dark piece of thread, we miss the big picture. But standing back and beholding the complete tapestry, we marvel at how the seemingly random pieces weave together to reveal a beautiful portrait. That's precisely what we must do with Joseph: Step back and see how the details of his life come together for a glorious purpose.

Joseph's life is a vital link in the grand narrative of redemption. He is the bridge between the Lord's covenant with Abraham and the nation of Israel, the people God chose to represent Him to the world. Joseph's ancestors are the patriarchs: Abraham, Isaac, and Jacob.

Recall God's promise in the Garden of Eden that the "Seed of the woman" would crush the Serpent. As Scripture unfolds, we discover that this victorious Seed (or human descendant of Adam and Eve) will come through Abraham's family line (see Gen. 12:1–3). Abraham had a son named Isaac, who had a son named Jacob. Jacob encountered the Lord, who then changed his name to Israel. Jacob had twelve sons, who founded the twelve tribes of Israel. But before we go down that family tree, let's look at Joseph.

Joseph's story is told in Genesis 37–50. He was beloved by his father, Jacob. He was gifted as a boy with prophetic dreams and even dreamed that his brothers would one day bow down before him. As a result, his envious brothers despised him. Fueled by jealousy, they seized him and sold him to slave traders who carried him to Egypt. Then they deceived their father, telling him that Joseph died at the paws of a wild animal.

Although Joseph was rejected by his family, sold as a slave, and falsely accused of a crime he didn't commit, Scripture repeatedly reminds us that "God was with Joseph." Through tumultuous twists and turns, he was kept by the hand of God. Then, when all seemed lost, the pharaoh of Egypt had a disturbing dream and needed someone to interpret it.

A former prison inmate remembered Joseph and told Pharaoh of his gift. Joseph not only gave the correct interpretation of the dream but offered Pharaoh valuable wisdom. As a result, Joseph moved from the prison to the palace and was given the top-ranking position in Egypt.

Holding royal authority, Joseph oversaw seven years of plenty and prepared Egypt for the seven years of starvation that he knew would come. His wise acquisition of grain enabled Egypt to withstand the famine. Then, driven by desperate hunger, his brothers traveled from Canaan to Egypt to find food.

Arriving in Egypt, Joseph's childhood dream came to fulfillment as his brothers prostrated themselves before him, begging for food. Although they did not recognize him, Joseph knew who they were. Through several encounters and interactions, he learned his father was still alive, and Joseph finally revealed his identity to his brothers.

Once the truth dawned on them, they were terrified. The very brother they sold into slavery was now the ruler of Egypt! In response to their fear, Joseph offered these famous words: "As for you, you meant evil against me, but God meant it for good, to bring it about that many people should be kept alive, as they are today" (Gen. 50:20 ESV).

Joseph was able to forgive because he recognized how the Lord permitted their envious acts for a sovereign purpose. The Lord sent him ahead to Egypt so that his entire family, the descendants of Abraham, would be saved from starvation.

After Joseph reconciled with his family, he invited Jacob's entire household to come to Egypt to live in the land of Goshen, where he provided for the family and their flocks. There, Abraham's descendants were protected from famine and began to multiply, just as the Lord promised.

Through Joseph's story we see the providence of God. What is providence? Here's a theological definition: Providence is the means by which God directs all things—both animate and inanimate, seen and unseen, good and evil—toward a worthy purpose, which means His will must finally prevail. As Pastor Tony Evans often says, "Providence is the hand of God in the glove of history."[1]

Through the meandering events of Joseph's life, we see the hand of God weaving threads of rejection, human deceit, lies, and a global crisis together for a divine purpose. God's intention to bless the world through a descendant of Abraham would not be thwarted by jealous brothers or a famine. What we discover as the Bible unfolds from garden to garden is the sovereignty of God, who alone can move the events of history toward His divine purpose.

Against the odds, God's people survive. Why? Because God was with Joseph. In the pit, the prison, and the palace, the Lord worked all things for Joseph's good and God's glory. And friend, He will do the same for you!

---

1 Tony Evans, https://go.tonyevans.org/blog/the-hand-of-providence.

*And we know that for those who love God all things work together for good, for those who are called according to his purpose.*

—Romans 8:28 ESV

## HARVEST

How has rejection, betrayal, or abandonment impacted your life? Maybe, like Joseph, you have threads of injustice weaving throughout your life story. What part of Joseph's life encourages you? Beloved, be encouraged that God wants to use those very things for your good and His glory! He knows and sees your heartache, and He can bring you out of the pit! Take your struggles and pain directly to the One who is both sovereign and faithful. Be assured that He sees you, He is with you, and He is right now working for your good.

DAY 9

# THE GREAT I AM

## SEED

*Then Moses said to God, "If I come to the people of Israel and say to them, 'The God of your fathers has sent me to you,' and they ask me, 'What is his name?' what shall I say to them?" God said to Moses, "I AM who I AM."*

—Exodus 3:13–14 ESV

## CULTIVATE

Read Exodus 1–3; Psalm 105.

## FLOURISH

I'll never forget the day I discovered I was pregnant. I was speaking at a women's conference when the telltale symptoms hit me. After racing from a pharmacy back to my hotel, I learned the thrilling news. At forty-three, I was what doctors call a "geriatric pregnancy." But I didn't take offense—I would finally be a mother!

Weeks later, my husband and I entered an ultrasound appointment to learn our baby's gender. Confident I was having a boy, I waited for confirmation. But to our surprise, the clinician said, "It's a girl!" Wonder of wonders! As soon as she uttered the words, I looked at Justin and exclaimed, "Her name is Sydney!"

This name was significant. Justin and I were in Sydney, Australia, when I was praying on the beach and the Lord impressed on my heart that we would have a baby. Months later, when we found out we were expecting, we named our daughter after the place where the promise was given.

Names are not only a big deal to expecting parents, but when it comes to the Bible, they carry great importance. In Scripture a person's name often signifies their character or calling. This proves especially true of God. Before Moses met the Lord at the burning bush, the Israelites called God "Elohim." This is a title, not a personal name. In the divine encounter we read today, God revealed not just His name, but His covenant identity.

In Exodus 1, we learn that after the Lord raised up Joseph to save his family from famine, they moved from Canaan to Egypt where they began to multiply. Unfortunately, the pharaohs who ruled after Joseph died did not look favorably upon the Israelites. As a result, the Hebrew people were enslaved—a far cry from the covenantal blessings handed down from their ancestors. How would these promises be realized when they were slaves?

Cue Moses.

Set apart at birth, God chose Moses as the deliverer to lead His people out of bondage (see Exod. 2:1–10). Although born a Hebrew child, he was raised in Pharaoh's home as a prince of Egypt. As a young man, Moses hated the oppression of his people and attempted to deliver them through his own strength by killing an Egyptian. But Moses' timing was not God's timing, and his method was not God's method. So after the killing of the Egyptian became known, Moses fled and lived for forty years in the wilderness as a shepherd.

The redemption story picks up in Exodus 3 where we find Moses tending sheep when something glorious captured his attention. Turning aside, he stopped to marvel at a burning bush. As he pondered the fiery sight, God said: "'Moses, Moses!' And he said, 'Here I am.' Then he said, 'Do not come near; take your sandals off your feet, for the place on which you are standing is holy ground'" (Exod. 3:4–5 ESV).

Holy ground. The place wasn't inherently holy but became so because God's Presence was there. God told Moses to take off his sandals, a sign of respect and humility. Moses' education began with first comprehending God's holiness. Biblical scholars use the word *otherly* to describe God's holiness because He is distinct from us. Therefore, Moses learned quickly that God's glorious Presence must be approached with great humility and according to divine instructions.

Moses encountered a holy God at the burning bush, but also a loving One. God told Moses that He saw the suffering of His people and was acting in response to their cries for help.

> *Then the LORD told him, "I have certainly seen the oppression of my people in Egypt. I have heard their cries of distress because of their harsh slave drivers. Yes, I am aware of their suffering. So I have come down to rescue them from the power of the Egyptians and lead them out of Egypt into their own fertile and spacious land. It is a land flowing with milk and honey."*
>
> —Exodus 3:7–8 NLT

Friend, hear this: God is the same yesterday, today, and forever. Yes, He is unquestionably holy, but He is also the God who runs into the fire to save His beloved…you are His beloved.

This dramatic encounter also reveals God's faithfulness. The Lord called Himself the God of Abraham, Isaac, and Jacob. He remembered the covenant promises He made and in response to their cry for help, He would deliver them from Egypt and bring them to the Promised Land (see Exod. 3:8–10).

This is terrific news, but long gone is the self-confident prince of Egypt who fancied himself a deliverer. This Moses is older, wiser, and aware of his inability. Therefore, he objected and asked: *How is this possible?*

God assured victory with one factor—"I will be with you" (Exod. 3:12 ESV). Who could compete with the Lord God Almighty? Neither Egypt's pharaoh nor any of their false gods were a threat. The Lord's Presence was all Moses needed to accomplish this task.

With that gracious guarantee, Moses asked one final question: "What if they ask me Your name?" You've got to admit it's a valid question. After all, Moses was marching back into a land proliferated with idols. In the ancient world, the name of a god encapsulated the essence, nature, and function of a deity. The "gods" of Egypt served specific functions, such as fertility, provision, or protection. Moses understood that the Hebrew people would want to know what sort of God was offering deliverance.

> *God said to Moses, "I AM WHO I AM." And he said, "Say this to the people of Israel: 'I AM has sent me to you.'" God also said to Moses, "Say this to the people of Israel: 'The LORD, the God of your fathers, the God of Abraham, the God of Isaac, and the God of Jacob, has sent me to you.' This is my name forever, and thus I am to be remembered throughout all generations."*
>
> —Exodus 3:14–15 ESV

He is the Great I AM! The Lord defined His identity as the self-existent, uncreated, all-powerful, infinite, eternal God Most High! I just love the fact that the Lord doesn't struggle with insecurity, nor does He have an identity crisis. With absolute certainty, He says, "I AM!" This covenant name expresses that He alone is

God. He has no rival, and He has no equal. Pastor John Piper sheds light on the importance of this name:

> Yahweh is God's proper name in Hebrew. The importance of it can be seen in the sheer frequency of its use. It occurs 6,828 times in the Old Testament. That's more than three times as often as the simple word for "God" (Elohim—2,600; El—238). What this fact shows is that God aims to be known not as a generic deity, but as a specific person with a name that carries his unique character and mission.[1]

It was based on God's promised Presence and in the power of His mighty name that Moses returned to Egypt on mission from Yahweh to deliver the Hebrew people from slavery. What the Lord promised to Abraham—the blessing of the world through his offspring—would come to pass. No Egyptian army or power of darkness could stand against the Great I AM!

Understanding the power of this name and the significance it held for the Jewish people becomes vital as we trace the redemption story from garden to garden. This name was so sacred to the Hebrew people that they wouldn't dare speak it or even write it. Therefore, the name *I AM* (or Yahweh) is translated throughout the Bible as "Lord" (in capital and small capital letters).

The burning bush encounter not only provided a revelation of God's holy name to Moses, but it also signified a turning point in redemptive history. Now the descendants of Abraham would become a special nation unto the Lord. But that's not all; this deliverance points forward to the ultimate deliverance. Just as God raised up Moses to deliver the Israelites from their physical slavery

---

1 John Piper, "I Am Who I Am," https://www.desiringgod.org/messages/i-am-who-i-am.

and lead them into the Promised Land, so He would one day send His Son, Jesus, as the ultimate Redeemer to free us from slavery to sin and death.

Friend, our God is faithful. He delivered His people from their bondage, and He can deliver you from anything that holds you captive today. Let His name, "I AM," remind you that there is nothing and no one greater or more powerful than your God!

> *But now thus says the LORD, he who created you, O Jacob, he who formed you, O Israel: "Fear not, for I have redeemed you; I have called you by name, you are mine."*
>
> —Isaiah 43:1 ESV

## HARVEST

We all, like Moses, have tried to accomplish things by our own strength and on our own timing. Are you like me, and often just take matters into your own hands when things get challenging? I know I need the reminder that the Most High God, the Great I AM, is the one leading me and working for my good. Do you need to focus on the Deliverer today rather than the struggle? Remind yourself that no power of darkness can stand against the Great I AM; that in your life there is nothing too daunting or strong that He cannot overcome it for you!

## DAY 10

# THE EXODUS

### SEED

*Say therefore to the people of Israel, "I am the LORD, and I will bring you out from under the burdens of the Egyptians, and I will deliver you from slavery to them, and I will redeem you with an outstretched arm and with great acts of judgment."*

—Exodus 6:6 ESV

### CULTIVATE

Read Exodus 11–12; Psalm 114.

### FLOURISH

Michelangelo's Sistine Chapel ceiling is one of the most famous pieces of art in the world. Trust me, it deserves the fanfare—it is a masterpiece! On several occasions, I've stood with my head tilted back to marvel at the ceiling. I'm always blown away by the minute detail and the artist's ability to portray the full redemption narrative using paint and plaster. Beginning with creation and concluding with the final judgment day, the focal point is the center fresco, where God is shown stretching out His finger to give life to the mortal Adam. Michelangelo is telling a story in which God takes center stage.

This scene captured my attention, for Michelangelo portrayed the Lord holding such power that He merely lifts a finger, and His will is done. This is not just the God of Michelangelo's imagination; this is the Lord God Almighty revealed on the pages of Scripture.

As we continue our survey of the Bible, we pause today to look at the exodus. Without exaggeration, it is impossible to understand the Bible without grasping this monumental moment in history. All other events and doctrines that follow point back to when the hand of God rescued His people.

We concluded yesterday with a revelation of God's holy name, Yahweh. He is the Great I AM, the eternal, self-existent God who has no rival! From the encounter at the burning bush, the Lord sent Moses back to Egypt to deliver the Israelites from bondage. At first Moses protested, but God promised His Presence would be with him, assuring their victory.

In Exodus chapters 5–10, we learn of Moses' confrontations with Pharaoh. Moses said, "Thus says the LORD, the God of Israel, 'Let my people go, that they may hold a feast to me in the wilderness.' But Pharaoh said, 'Who is the LORD, that I should obey his voice and let Israel go? I do not know the LORD, and moreover, I will not let Israel go'" (Exod. 5:1–2 ESV).

The crux of the showdown that follows is Pharaoh's question: "Who is the Lord that I should obey Him?" While Pharaoh belittled the Lord, God thundered back with ten miraculous wonders (or plagues against Egypt). Through these plagues, His glorious power over the so-called gods of Egypt was on full display.

*The Nile River turned to blood.*

*Frogs, gnats, and flies covered the land.*

*Livestock perished.*

*Boils formed.*

*Hail destroyed crops.*

*Swarming locusts consumed what remained.*

*Then a heavy darkness so thick that it could be felt descended on Egypt.*

As the standoff dragged on, the plagues became more severe, but God's people were protected. Then Pharaoh's magicians said, "This is the finger of God" (Exod. 8:19 ESV). They knew they were outmatched. Yahweh held more power in His finger than all the collective idols of Egypt. But even with mounting evidence, Pharaoh's heart was hardened, and "he would not listen to them, as the LORD had said" (8:19 ESV).

Finally, we come to the tenth and final plague. In Scripture, the number ten often symbolizes completeness. This one would be the ultimate sign of God's authority and bring Pharaoh to his knees. This plague was the death of the firstborn.

God warned Moses that the angel of death would pass over Egypt and every firstborn would die—from the poorest servant to the prince in Pharaoh's palace—none were exempt from this plague. But before it happened, the Lord gave specific instructions about how to be saved from it.

God told the Israelites to take a lamb into their homes and inspect it for five days to guarantee it was perfect. Then the father was to take the lamb, sacrifice it, and mark their doorframes with its blood. Then, when the Lord passed through Egypt, He would "pass over" households marked by the blood (see Exod. 12:21–23).

> *The blood shall be a sign for you, on the houses where you are. And when I see the blood, I will pass over you, and no plague will befall you to destroy you, when I strike the land of Egypt.*
>
> —Exodus 12:13 ESV

By faith the Israelites sacrificed their lambs and placed the blood on their doorframes—on the top, sides, and bottom. Once again, a sacrifice spills blood to give life to another. As the lambs were offered, their blood marked the doorframes and those inside were protected from the plague. If they were to step back, they would see the shape of a cross painted in blood.

Simply by trusting God's word and following His method of deliverance they were saved. When the angel of death passed through the land of Egypt that fateful night, those covered by the blood of the lamb were spared, but those who refused to heed God's warning experienced death.

By the next morning, Pharaoh and the Egyptians begged the Israelites to leave. With this final plague, their captor relented and let God's people go. Armed with plunder of silver and gold and with their children and belongings in tow, the Hebrew people made a mass exodus out of Egypt.

A few days later however, Egypt's pharaoh regretted losing the Israelites as his free labor source, so he called for his chariots to chase them down (see Exod. 14:5–12). Put yourself in Israel's sandals for a second: One minute you are free, but the next minute your old slave master is trying to take you back to captivity.

But the Red Sea stood before the Israelites, mountains surrounded them, and now the most powerful army in the world was at their heels. With nowhere to run, fear gripped the people as they watched Pharaoh's mighty army drawing near.

Amid the panic, Moses told the Israelites, "Fear not, stand firm, and see the salvation of the LORD, which he will work for you today" (Exod. 14:13 ESV). Despite the overwhelming obstacles, Moses believed the Lord would deliver them. Moses stood firm in faith and watched as the Lord worked a miracle. God told Moses to stretch out his staff, and as he did, the Red Sea parted before him, creating a highway of dry land for Israel to cross (see Exod. 14:15–22).

Friend, our God is not bound by the laws of nature—for He is the Lord of all creation! The sea obeyed its Maker and parted before the Israelites' eyes! This miracle sealed their deliverance from Egypt. Then after they crossed the Red Sea, Pharaoh's army rushed in behind them and was utterly wiped away as the sea flooded their path. The Lord God Almighty delivered His people!

Yahweh was faithful to keep His promises. He led them out of slavery to lead them into the Promised Land, and His very Presence was their guide. As the Lord established them as a nation, He changed their identity from slaves to sons and daughters of God. One aspect of their national identity was to look back each year and celebrate the Feast of Passover to remember how "the Lord brought us out of Egypt with a mighty hand and an outstretched arm" (Deut. 26:8 ESV).

This epoch deliverance pointed forward to the ultimate Redeemer, Jesus Christ. He is the Lamb of God whose blood was poured out on a cross to deliver us from our slavery to sin and break the curse of death.

Scripture teaches that Jesus' death was intentional. To be precise, before the foundation of the world, a divine decision was made. In order for your sin and my sin to be passed over, the perfect covering was required. And we will discover as this incredible story unfolds from garden to garden that it was the precious blood of Jesus that paid our ransom. Just think, when the Lord stretched out His hand as our Redeemer, He did so to take hold of yours!

> *Knowing that you were ransomed from the futile ways inherited from your forefathers, not with perishable things such as silver or gold, but with the precious blood of Christ, like that of a lamb without blemish or spot. He was foreknown before the foundation of the world but was made manifest in the last times for the sake of you who through him are believers in God, who raised him from the dead and gave him glory, so that your faith and hope are in God.*
>
> —1 Peter 1:18–21 ESV

## HARVEST

At some point in our lives, even if subconsciously, we have all asked ourselves the same question that Pharaoh did: "Who is the Lord, that I should obey His voice?" How we answer the question of "*Who* is the Lord?" is foundational to how we respond to God. Do you know God as the Great I AM...the Lord God Almighty? Is following His commands something that brings you delight or do you reject His authority like Pharaoh? Surrendering to God proves sweet when we meditate on the sacrificial love that He displayed for us in sending His Son as our Deliverer. Take time today to allow the truth of Jesus' sacrifice for you to lead your heart to full surrender to God's will.

— DAY 11 —

# THE TEN COMMANDMENTS

## SEED

*You yourselves have seen what I did to the Egyptians, and how I bore you on eagles' wings and brought you to myself. Now therefore, if you will indeed obey my voice and keep my covenant, you shall be my treasured possession among all peoples, for all the earth is mine; and you shall be to me a kingdom of priests and a holy nation.*

—Exodus 19:4–6 ESV

## CULTIVATE

Read Exodus 19–20; Matthew 22:36–40.

## FLOURISH

It was late Christmas night when our normal bedtime routine became holy ground. The presents were unwrapped, our bellies were full, and our bodies were weary from a day of festivities when I finally tucked my daughter into bed. Little ones try their best at Christmas to avoid the infamous naughty list, but even with their best efforts, they mess up and need grace. Sydney and I were halfway through her bedtime prayers when she stopped me to share something that had been weighing heavy on her little heart. She felt guilty and ashamed for something she'd done. Then, with tears streaming down her face, she told me the whole story.

As her momma, I had a choice to make. I could either take this moment to teach my child the Gospel (the true reason we give gifts at Christmas), or I could leave her burdened with guilt and shame without knowing how to be free. Although I was bone tired, I knew this was an opportunity to teach her the difference between good behavior and the Gospel.

Good behavior focuses on the rules, demanding, "Do better. Try harder to be good. Hide your imperfections. And don't dare mess up or you'll be on the naughty list." On the other hand, the Gospel of grace tells us, "Yes, you messed up because you are a sinner. But here is the Good News: Jesus Christ came to save sinners just like me and you. And when we confess our mistakes and trust Jesus as our Savior, He will forgive us. But He doesn't just stop there; Jesus gives us new hearts so that we can be like Him."

I agreed with Sydney that her actions were wrong but explained that she could pray to God and receive His grace. I told her the Good News that Jesus died in her place so she could be forgiven. While she was years away from comprehending the Gospel's fullness, my prayer as I tucked her in was that she would understand that God loves her, and that only Jesus can take away her burden of guilt and shame.

I'm sharing the difference between good behavior and the Gospel to illustrate the two radically different ways people interpret God's holy law in the Bible. Good behavior looks at the law as a checklist of rules to obey, but the Gospel looks at God's holy law like a mirror, which reveals our desperate need for grace that forgives our sins and transforms us from the inside out. Knowing the difference between good behavior and the Gospel of grace is fundamental to interpreting today's focal passage.

*For no one can ever be made right with God by doing what the law commands. The law simply shows us how sinful we are.*

—Romans 3:20 NLT

Yesterday, we learned how the Lord delivered His people from slavery in Egypt through the sacrifice of the Passover Lamb and the dramatic parting of the Red Sea. As we continue our survey of the Bible from garden to garden, we now come to the base of Mount Sinai, where one of the most critical events in human history occurred. It was here that the Lord established His covenant with the nation of Israel and gave them the Ten Commandments.

Then, three months after leaving Egypt, the Hebrew people finally arrived at Mount Sinai (the same place where Moses had first encountered the Lord at the burning bush). The Lord brought them to this mountain because He wanted to establish a covenant with Israel—and from this point on, they would be "a kingdom of priests and a holy nation" (Exod. 19:6 ESV).

It's important to note that unlike the everlasting and unconditional covenant blessings God promised Abraham (see Gen. 12:1–3), the covenant God made with the nation of Israel at Mount Sinai was conditional. Meaning, this one required Israel's faithfulness to the Lord and they had a part to play in the relationship. When told the requirements, the people responded joyfully, "All that the LORD has spoken we will do" (Exod. 19:8 ESV).

Three days after they made this promise, the Lord appeared in a dense cloud on Mount Sinai, accompanied by thunder, trumpet blasts, and lightning. Moses told the people to stand at the base as the Lord descended in fire and declared to them the Ten Commandments (see Exod. 20:2–17). These statutes revealed God's standard of holiness and how they were to live as His covenant people.

- You shall have no other gods before Me.
- You shall not make for yourself an idol in the form of anything.
- You shall not misuse the name of the Lord your God.
- Remember the Sabbath day by keeping it holy.
- Honor your father and mother.
- You shall not murder.
- You shall not commit adultery.
- You shall not steal.
- You shall not lie.
- You shall not covet.

This powerful scene could be compared to a marriage ceremony. God and Israel met at Mount Sinai, where they exchanged vows. Now Israel belonged to the Lord and God promised to bless them if they kept the covenant. Hearing God's voice thunder from Sinai, the Israelites trembled in His Presence and again vowed, "All the words that the LORD has spoken we will do" (Exod. 24:3 ESV).

Now this is where the story gets depressing. God called Moses back up the mountain to give him two tablets on which He wrote the Ten Commandments. Moses remained there for forty days, so long in fact that the people feared he wouldn't return. In his absence, Israel's devotion to the Lord and commitment to the covenant were tested. As the days passed, their restlessness grew, and they longed for the familiar things they knew in Egypt. They conspired with Aaron, Moses' brother, to build an idol, a golden calf. This idolatry was a great rebellion against the Lord.

Sadly, the people broke their vow to keep the covenant before Moses even returned with the Ten Commandments engraved on stone tablets. When Moses eventually came down the mountain, he saw the people worshipping the golden calf and became so angry that he crushed the tablets.

It's crazy to think that even though Israel had beheld Yahweh's glory in the cloud and trembled at His voice, they still fashioned an idol after something they knew in Egypt. Why did they do this? Better yet, why do any of us do this?

Tim Keller rightly diagnosed the problem: "The human heart is an idol factory that takes good things like a successful career, love, material possessions, even family, and turns them into ultimate things. Our hearts deify them as the center of our lives, because, we think, they can give us significance and security, safety and fulfillment, if we attain them."[1]

The Israelites broke their covenant vow, yet Moses pleaded with God to forgive their sin. And the God of second chances graciously forgave their rebellion and engraved the covenant again on stone tablets for them to keep.

Their idolatry points to humanity's great problem—God's law written on stone can't change our sinful condition. While the Ten Commandments are beautiful, right, and intended for human flourishing, the problem doesn't lie with God's law; the problem is with our rebel hearts. Thankfully, what is "impossible with men is possible with God" (Luke 18:27 ESV).

As we proceed through the Old Testament, we see sin's consequences written in bold across the pages of history. The nation of Israel continually worshipped idols and rejected Yahweh. Centuries later, after countless second chances, God's people would

---

1 Tim Keller, *Counterfeit Gods: The Empty Promises of Money, Sex, and Power, and the Only Hope That Matters* (New York: Penguin, 2011), xiv.

become prisoners again in a land called Babylon. The reason this happened was because they broke the covenant, which stipulated lavish blessings if they kept it, but warned they would be removed from their land and handed over to their enemies if they did not (see Deut. 28).

Even though their captivity was a result of their rebellion, the Lord still offered a beacon of hope. God raised up prophets who foretold that God would establish a New Covenant, and unlike the old one that could be broken by human sin, this one would be unbreakable because it would be perfectly fulfilled by God and written on our hearts instead of on stone! (See Jer. 31:31–34.)

This hope of an unbreakable, everlasting covenant is the Good News that Jesus Christ offers. Sin has reigned in every human heart since the Garden of Eden. Like Israel, instead of worshipping the Lord, our affections are given to lesser things. We lie, cheat, steal, covet, and hurt each other to get our way. The Law of God, while good and glorious, can't change our fallen condition; it is just a mirror that reveals our brokenness.

Religions around the world are built on keeping a list of rules and behavior modification, but those systems don't bring the soul peace or give the gift of eternal life—only a relationship with God established on His amazing grace does that. I lived far too long believing the lie that I had to perform perfectly to earn God's love, but now I know that only the Gospel of grace brings freedom from guilt and shame.

This is the beauty of the New Covenant—it would not be engraved on stone, but upon our hearts. Friend, Jesus ushered in this New Covenant with His sacrificial death and resurrection. When we put our hope in Him, we can stand faultless before God because Jesus takes away our sin and in turn, we take on His perfect righteousness. Not only that, but He gives us a new heart that desires to please God. And He gives us the Holy Spirit, who empowers us to live for His glory!

Friend, that's what I call Good News!

> *I will give you a new heart, and a new spirit I will put within you. And I will remove the heart of stone from your flesh and give you a heart of flesh. And I will put my Spirit within you, and cause you to walk in my statutes and be careful to obey my rules.*
>
> —Ezekiel 36:26–27 ESV

## HARVEST

Is your life characterized more by good behavior or the Gospel of grace? Are you motivated more by God's love for you or by fear of not measuring up? Take a minute to reflect on the Ten Commandments and allow the mirror of God's holy law to show you how much you need the grace of God and the power of God to change. Ask the Lord to change anything in you from the inside out and give you a heart that reflects His.

## DAY 12

# THE TABERNACLE

### SEED

*And let them make me a sanctuary, that I may dwell in their midst. Exactly as I show you concerning the pattern of the tabernacle, and of all its furniture, so you shall make it.*

—Exodus 25:8–9 ESV

### CULTIVATE

Read Exodus 40; Psalm 84; Hebrews 9.

### FLOURISH

No one warned me when I boarded a flight for London that I would absolutely fall in love with English gardens. As a woman who'd read every Jane Austen novel that she could get her hands on, there were many things I expected to enjoy about England, but by far, what captured my affection most were the gardens. Rich with color, overflowing with florals, and featuring quaint benches nestled under canopies of shade—the Brits know how to create beautiful landscapes.

My love for an English garden first bloomed during a seminary study abroad program at the University of Oxford. My time there was life-changing and could be likened to a "burning bush" experience. No, I did not see the Lord in a flaming azalea shrub, but I did sense Jesus calling me into my specific ministry. My summer in England was marked by a real sense of God's nearness and goodness.

As I reflect on the days I spent reading, praying, and walking the grounds surrounding Oxford, I believe that is the closest to the Garden of Eden I've ever felt. I communed with the Lord while enveloped in beautiful gardens.

As we progress through the Bible from garden to garden, we face the harsh reality that humanity is no longer in Eden. The weeds of sin, shame, and blame grow wild in the human heart. But the longing for Eden, our true home, always remains. We know that we were created for something glorious, something beautiful, something distinguished by the Presence of God.

As the Bible unfolds, we cling to the promise He gave in Eden that the "Seed of the woman" would crush the head of the Serpent, bringing divine restoration. The Lord is faithful to His promises, and through the pages of Scripture we see how God made a way for us to be with Him. This redemption story includes signs, symbols, and specific imagery designed to point our way back into relationship with God. One primary example was God's instruction to Israel to build a tabernacle, where He could dwell among them.

All of God's Word bears importance, but when more than fifty chapters are devoted to the subject of the tabernacle, we are wise to pay attention. When Moses met with the Lord on Mount Sinai, he was given the Law. Additionally, God showed Moses heavenly blueprints—the design for a sanctuary where the Lord would once again dwell with His people. Every detail of this tabernacle was designed to evoke images of Eden and pointed the way back into God's Presence.

The Lord told Moses to build the tabernacle and place it in the middle of the Israelites with the twelve tribes camped around it. This signified that their identity as a people centered on Yahweh.

Just as in the Garden of Eden, where Adam and Eve walked with God, so Israel would experience life with God at the center.

A white linen fence symbolizing God's holiness surrounded the tabernacle. Inside this fence was an outer courtyard, and then the tent that contained two rooms: the Holy Place and the Holy of Holies.

There was only one access point to the tabernacle, a gate located on the eastern side of the outer court. Just as Adam and Eve left the Garden of Eden through the east and the way was guarded by a flaming sword, this tabernacle's eastern face symbolized the "one way" back into God's Presence.

God ordained for priests to serve in the tabernacle. The high priest stood before God as a representative of the nation. He would make sacrifices and offer prayers on behalf of the people. As the priest entered the outer court, he first encountered an altar for sacrifices and a laver for cleansing. The book of Leviticus explains the sacrificial system in great detail and how those offerings atoned for sin and provided a way to worship the Lord.

As the priest proceeded from the courtyard into the tent, he first entered the Holy Place. This space was adorned with a golden lampstand, a table of shewbread, and an altar of incense. As an Israelite peered into this Holy Place, they would see colors, tapestries, and images of a garden paradise. In vivid color and with lavish detail, each element was designed to look like the Garden of Eden. As the priest entered the Holy Place, his eyes would fasten on the great golden lampstand that was intentionally designed to represent the Tree of Life in the middle of Eden.

Passing through the Holy Place, the priest then encountered a veil. This curtain blocked the way into the Holy of Holies, where God's glory rested above the Mercy Seat and the Ark of the Covenant. Access to the Holy of Holies was only given to the high priest, once a year, on the Day of Atonement. There, the high priest would stand before the cloud of God's glory that filled the Holy of Holies.

This cloud was the Shekinah glory, which led Israel throughout their journey from Egypt to the Promised Land. During the day, the cloud sheltered them from the brutal desert sun; at night, it burned as a pillar of fire (see Exod. 13:21–22). Exodus describes the awesome moment when God's glory filled the tabernacle:

> *Then the cloud covered the tent of meeting, and the glory of the LORD filled the tabernacle. And Moses was not able to enter the tent of meeting because the cloud settled on it, and the glory of the LORD filled the tabernacle.*
>
> —40:34–35 ESV

During their arduous forty-year wilderness journey and throughout the conquest of the Promised Land, the tabernacle served as the center of Israel's worship of Yahweh. It was the Presence of Yahweh, the Great I AM, in the midst of His people that made this tent sacred. Without God's Presence it was nothing. Many years later, during the reign of King Solomon, the tabernacle was replaced by the Temple in Jerusalem. Although this Temple was far more glamorous, the structure and symbolism of Eden was the same. And just as the Shekinah glory filled the tabernacle, the cloud filled the Holy of Holies in the Temple.

A book that has marked my life is *The Pursuit of God* by A. W. Tozer. In this soul-searching work, Tozer reminds us that the greatest need of the human heart is to abide in the very Presence of God as Adam and Eve did in Eden. We are wired for this connection and all of Scripture reveals the way back home.

> The interior journey of the soul from the wilds of sin into the enjoyed Presence of God is beautifully illustrated in the

> Old Testament tabernacle...While the tabernacle stood, only the high priest could enter there, and that but once a year, with blood which he offered for his sins and the sins of the people...
>
> Everything in the New Testament accords with the Old Testament picture. Ransomed men need no longer to pause in fear to enter the Holy of Holies. God wills that we should push on into His Presence and live our whole life there. This is to be known to us in conscious experience. It is more than a doctrine to be held, it is a life to be enjoyed every moment of every day.[1]

The design of the Old Testament tabernacle was intended to point the way back to the Garden of Eden, into the Presence of God. The elements and layout of the tabernacle taught the Israelites that the way back into God's Presence was not through keeping the Law, but through sacrifice. Each lamb offered at the altar pointed forward to Jesus Christ, who would offer His life as the ultimate sacrifice (see Heb. 4:14–16). And the high priest, who entered the Holy of Holies each year to represent the people before Holy God, pointed forward to Jesus, our Great High Priest who stands today as our Redeemer.

> *But when Christ appeared as a high priest of the good things that have come, then through the greater and more perfect tent (not made with hands, that is, not of this creation) he entered once for all into the holy places, not by means of the blood of goats and calves but by means of his own blood, thus securing an eternal redemption.*
>
> —Hebrews 9:11–12 ESV

---

1 Tozer, *Pursuit of God*, 36–37.

## HARVEST

Because Jesus Christ is the Great High Priest over the house of God, we no longer need a sacrifice or a priest to atone for our sins. God's Word tells us we can approach His throne confidently and experience His grace in our time of need. How do you need God's grace today? What burden, trouble, struggles, or sin do you need to carry to the Lord? Be encouraged, for the Lord says to you, "Come boldly" (Heb. 4:16 NKJV). Friend, this is your invitation to run to God's throne of grace!

DAY 13

# THE PROMISED LAND

## SEED

*No man shall be able to stand before you all the days of your life. Just as I was with Moses, so I will be with you. I will not leave you or forsake you. Be strong and courageous, for you shall cause this people to inherit the land that I swore to their fathers to give them.*

—Joshua 1:56 ESV

## CULTIVATE

Read Joshua 1; 21:43–45.

## FLOURISH

I've traveled to Israel on many occasions, and the clichés about the Holy Land are true—the Bible does indeed come alive when you walk where Jesus walked. While there are many must-see spots that most tourist groups check off their lists, one of my favorite historical sites is off the beaten path.

I'm speaking of Mount Nebo, which rises more than four thousand feet above the Dead Sea on the east side of the Jordan River. I love this place for many reasons. First, Mount Nebo offers a stunning panoramic view of the Promised Land. After all, this is the very spot where the Lord brought Moses to give him a look at the land before he died (see Num. 27:12). Although Moses would not enter in, he could see all the way to Jerusalem from this vantage point.

I also love visiting this overlook because it represents the transition from Moses' leadership of God's people to Joshua's, a man who takes the mantle of responsibility to possess the Promised Land.

We pick up Joshua's story forty years after the mighty hand of God rescued the Israelites from Egypt and they had finally arrived on the precipice of inheriting the land promised to their ancestors—Abraham, Isaac, and Jacob. The Lord described the land as "flowing with milk and honey" (Exod. 3:8 ESV), which meant it was fertile and flourishing—the exact opposite of the barren wilderness that had been their home for forty years.

Taking possession of their inheritance came four decades later than expected. The generation whom God redeemed from slavery arrived at the point of occupying the land, but they didn't obtain the blessing. What kept them from entering the Promised Land? One word—*fear*!

After the exodus, Israel spent two years camped at Mount Sinai, where God established them as a nation. Then they set out for the Promised Land. God told Moses to send twelve spies, one representative of each tribe of Israel, to survey the land (see Num. 13:1–3). Among them were two men of great faith, Caleb and Joshua. Moses dispatched the twelve with a mission to report about the land's inhabitants and defense systems and bring back produce samples.

Forty days later, the spies returned with ample evidence of the land's fruitfulness: figs, pomegranates, and massive clusters of grapes. The land was indeed flowing with milk and honey! Despite this bounty, ten of the spies (excluding Caleb and Joshua) spread doubt throughout the Israelites by telling them that they could not possibly take the land because it was filled with giants.

Fear spread and infected every family in every tribe. Rather than focusing on the promises of God, they focused on the size of their enemy. Caleb stood up and encouraged the people to believe the Lord. He believed that with God's help they could take the land. Caleb said, "Let us go up at once and occupy it, for we are well able to overcome it" (Num. 13:30 ESV). Unfortunately, the other spies instilled such terror that the whole nation cried out, "Would that we had died in the land of Egypt! Or would that we had died in this wilderness!"(Num. 14:1–2 ESV).

Fear proves to be faith in the Enemy and blinds us to the Presence of God with us! The Lord who redeemed them from slavery was the same God leading them to take possession of their inheritance. Because of their unbelief, that generation did not possess the Promised Land. Their children would take possession under the leadership of Joshua, the other spy who believed God's promises.

Forty years of wandering in the wilderness had passed when Joshua took the leadership mantle after Moses' death. Those were mighty big sandals to fill, but the Lord assured him, "Every place that the sole of your foot will tread upon I have given to you" (Josh. 1:3 ESV). The Promised Land was guaranteed—all that was required was faith. Yahweh was with Joshua and Israel took possession of the land promised to Abraham, Isaac, and Jacob.

From garden to garden, the Bible is one story. Every person, event, and promise points us to Jesus, who leads us into our spiritual Promised Land. And Joshua, the man chosen to lead Israel into their Promised Land, is a key figure in this redemption story. Recall that names in the Bible hold great significance. Joshua's name is *Yeshua* in Hebrew and means "Yahweh saves." And get this, the name *Yeshua* is translated as "Jesus" in English.

To pull these pieces together, press pause on Israel's journey into their Promised Land and fast-forward to the birth of Christ, when an angel appeared to Mary explaining that she would bear the Son of God. Her fiancé, Joseph, was told, "She will bear a son, and you shall call his name Jesus, for he will save his people from their sins" (Matt. 1:21 ESV).

It's not by chance that Jesus (Yeshua) was the name chosen for God's Son. The Lord was connecting the physical deliverance of the Israelites with the spiritual deliverance of all who hope in Jesus as their Redeemer.

Joshua was chosen by God to lead the people of Israel into their physical inheritance and give them victory over their enemies. His life embodied the message "Yahweh saves!" Likewise, Jesus Christ, who is the greater Joshua (Yeshua), leads us into our spiritual inheritance and gives us victory over our enemies—Satan, sin, and death.

There's another reason the Son of God was given this name. There was another important Joshua in the Old Testament. He served as the high priest in the Temple after God's people returned from the Babylonian exile (more on that story later). In a vision, the prophet Zechariah saw Joshua, a high priest crowned with majesty, seated on a throne, and charged with building God's Temple. This vision is a detailed prophecy concerning Jesus Christ, who is the Priestly King building the true Temple of God!

Both men in the Old Testament given the name Joshua pointed forward to Jesus, our Great High Priest who saves us and leads us to our spiritual Promised Land. He rules from heaven in majesty as King of Kings and Lord of Lords. Only in Jesus do all these prophetic pieces come together in the One whose name means "Jehovah is salvation"!

Friend, as we reflect on the Israelites' hesitation to step into their Promised Land, we must pause and evaluate how the same root of fear grows in our hearts as well. We conquer our fears with faith as we meditate on Jesus, our Savior, and the divine plan of God to lead us out of spiritual slavery and into our own inheritance. We fix our spiritual eyes of faith on...

- the One who keeps His promises;
- the One who empowers us for the journey;
- the One who will never leave us or forsake us.

Victory is our inheritance in Christ. The abundant life in Jesus is promised to those who take hold of Him by faith. Therefore, let's resist the temptation to shrink back in fear and believe God for all that He's promised us in Christ.

> *Blessed be the God and Father of our Lord Jesus Christ, who has blessed us in Christ with every spiritual blessing in the heavenly places...In him we have obtained an inheritance, having been predestined according to the purpose of him who works all things according to the counsel of his will, so that we who were the first to hope in Christ might be to the praise of his glory.*
>
> —Ephesians 1:3, 11–12 ESV

## HARVEST

Is there something that God is calling you to step into, your own Promised Land? Do you find yourself being held back by fear? Friend, *fear not*—just as God was with the Israelites and made the way for them, He will do that for you. He will be with you and never leave you. He keeps His promises, and He will equip you for your task. Take time today to dream with God about the call and purpose of your life and where He is leading you.

## DAY 14

# THE SHEPHERD KING

### SEED

*So David prevailed over the Philistine with a sling and with a stone, and struck the Philistine and killed him. There was no sword in the hand of David. Then David ran and stood over the Philistine and took his sword and drew it out of its sheath and killed him and cut off his head with it. When the Philistines saw that their champion was dead, they fled.*

—1 Samuel 17:50–51 ESV

### CULTIVATE

Read 1 Samuel 16–17; Psalm 100.

### FLOURISH

David vs. Goliath is a legendary tale that fuels the imagination of both children and adults. It's the anthem of the underdog, an unlikely hero who walks away a champion. In this famous saga, we find a story hidden within a story. David was a shepherd boy who became the greatest king of Israel. Yet in examining his great faith, we discover that the battle between David and Goliath foreshadows the ultimate showdown between the "Seed of the woman" and the Serpent!

Hundreds of years after the twelve tribes of Israel settled into the Promised Land under Joshua's leadership, God's covenant people were in a sad cycle of rebellion and bondage. They turned away from the Lord, and as a result they were oppressed by their enemies. This constant struggle gave rise to a request—they asked God for a king like all the other nations had.

Although Israel was established by God as a theocracy, whereby Yahweh was their King, Provider, and Defender, they desired an earthly ruler. The Lord gave in to their request and anointed Saul as king. Although Saul looked the part, his heart was not devoted to the Lord. Saul rebelled against God, and the Lord removed the kingdom from him. God said to the prophet Samuel:

> *Do not look on his appearance or on the height of his stature, because I have rejected him. For the LORD sees not as man sees: man looks on the outward appearance, but the LORD looks on the heart.*
>
> —1 Samuel 16:7 ESV

The Lord then sent Samuel to Bethlehem to anoint a son of Jesse from the tribe of Judah as king. David was the youngest and the least likely to be picked for the role. He spent his time tending his father's sheep. Yet, when Samuel went to Bethlehem, the Lord didn't choose one of his brothers. Instead, God said about the young shepherd, David, "Arise, anoint him; for this is the one!" (1 Sam. 16:12 NKJV).

Although David was anointed, it would be nearly two decades before he wore the crown. In the meantime, Israel was under the failing leadership of the cowardly King Saul.

This brings us to the showdown between Israel and the Philistines, who were led by Goliath—a giant with a loud mouth equal to his size. Goliath boasted of his victories and continually taunted Israel. Then he issued a challenge: Israel could choose a champion to represent them and face him in battle. If that man killed Goliath, then the Philistines would become Israel's servants. But if Goliath won, then Israel would become their slaves.

Think of this challenge like the Olympics. When athletes compete, they represent the whole nation. If they win, their country wins gold. Likewise, when Goliath called for a champion, the nation's destiny was wrapped up in whoever faced the giant. No one in Israel's army was willing to step forward. King Saul quaked in fear, and under his leadership, the military did the same.

Cue David.

As the standoff lingered, David's father sent him from tending the sheep to the front lines to check on his brothers who served under King Saul. When he arrived, David heard Goliath's taunts and challenges. Incensed at the audacity of the Philistine to mock the Living God, David volunteered to serve as Israel's champion.

The contrast between Saul and David is striking—one cowered in fear, and the other was emboldened by faith in God. King Saul looked at this showdown from a human perspective and reasoned no one could stand against Goliath. But David looked at this showdown from a heavenly perspective and figured that if God was with him, he couldn't lose! David said to Saul:

> *"Your servant used to keep sheep for his father. And when there came a lion, or a bear, and took a lamb from the flock, I went after him and struck him and delivered it out of his mouth. And if he arose against me, I caught him by his beard and struck him and killed him. Your servant has struck down both*

*lions and bears, and this uncircumcised Philistine shall be like one of them, for he has defied the armies of the living God." And David said, "The LORD who delivered me from the paw of the lion and from the paw of the bear will deliver me from the hand of this Philistine." And Saul said to David, "Go, and the LORD be with you!"*

—1 Samuel 17:34–37 ESV

David believed, "God's got this!" Which is precisely what he proclaimed as he stepped forward to face Goliath. David's faith in Yahweh believed He would bring the victory.

*Then David said to the Philistine, "You come to me with a sword and with a spear and with a javelin, but I come to you in the name of the LORD of hosts, the God of the armies of Israel, whom you have defied. This day the LORD will deliver you into my hand, and I will strike you down and cut off your head. And I will give the dead bodies of the host of the Philistines this day to the birds of the air and to the wild beasts of the earth, that all the earth may know that there is a God in Israel, and that all this assembly may know that the LORD saves not with sword and spear. For the battle is the LORD's, and he will give you into our hand."*

—1 Samuel 17:45–47 ESV

With his words echoing across the battlefield, what happened next went down in the history books. Taking out five smooth stones and a slingshot, the young shepherd king hurled a rock that struck like a bullet between Goliath's eyes. That big-talking giant fell with a thud, and the future king of Israel rushed to the fallen champion and cut off his head.

David's victory was Israel's victory. As their champion, he represented his people and won the day! This is far more than a story about a young kid who slew a giant. Taking a step back, we see the bigger story of the Bible. Just as Israel could not defeat their enemy, we are in the same predicament. King David foreshadowed Jesus, our Champion.

Jesus was a direct descendant of King David, fulfilling God's promise that from David's line would come a new king, who would reign forever and build a new Eden—a Temple for God's Presence (see 1 Chron. 17:11–14). Perfectly fulfilling this prophecy, Jesus was born in Bethlehem (David's hometown) and was anointed by the Holy Spirit as the King of Glory. Like David, Jesus even called Himself the "good shepherd" (John 10:11 ESV) who came to lay down His life for His sheep.

Our hope is not found in being strong enough to fight our battles. Our confidence in facing our enemies is the same that emboldened King David. We stand against our giants by trusting, "God's got this!"

Jesus is our Champion, the ultimate Shepherd King, who defeated our Goliath—Satan himself. At the cross, Jesus died in our place as our Champion, and with His resurrection, He crushed the head of the Serpent, fulfilling God's promise to Adam and Eve in the Garden of Eden. The victory of Jesus, the Shepherd King, is our victory! And His triumph brings our freedom!

> *But thanks be to God, who gives us the victory*
> *through our Lord Jesus Christ.*
>
> —1 Corinthians 15:57 ESV

## HARVEST

We have all faced giants in our lives, and perhaps you are facing one now. Do you believe, as David did, that "God's got this!"? If the Lord has led you into this situation, then the battle is His! And looking at the bigger picture, take some time to praise the Shepherd King, who defeated our enemy of death on the cross. We can live with peace and confidence of the future, because no matter what battles we face, ultimate victory belongs to Jesus our King!

## — DAY 15 —

# THE PROPHETS' HOPE

### — SEED

*For I know the plans I have for you, declares the LORD, plans for welfare and not for evil, to give you a future and a hope.*

—Jeremiah 29:11 ESV

### — CULTIVATE

Read Isaiah 61; Jeremiah 31:31–34.

### — FLOURISH

When a friend texted recently, I didn't need to read more than a few sentences to discern discouragement in her heart. She said, "Marian, I'm reaching out because I know you get it. I'm not sure I can handle waiting anymore." She shared her frustration and fears concerning singleness and how she was beginning to lose hope.

You see, my friend is waiting on God for marriage. She is beautiful, talented, and loves Jesus. Still, she is beginning to feel like a carton of milk with a looming expiration date. Looking around her community, she doesn't see prospects for a potential husband, and she's struggling to hope.

Her words brought back vivid memories of my painful waiting season. Years seemed to drag by when I was single, watching others find love and live "happily ever after." I remember fighting feelings of rejection and feeling forgotten by God.

My friend was right. I do get it—waiting is hard. But it's not just something single people do as they wait on God for a spouse. We all experience unmet desires. I have friends waiting on God for children, others for career doors to open, and some for physical healing.

Waiting is a barren place where what we believe about God is tested. Thankfully, the Bible is filled with men and women who had to watch, pray, and wait for promises from God to be fulfilled. These saints waited with eyes fixed on God's faithfulness. One such man was the prophet Jeremiah, who reminded his heart not to give up hope during some of the darkest days God's people ever faced:

> *The thought of my suffering and homelessness is bitter beyond words.*
> *I will never forget this awful time, as I grieve over my loss.*
> *Yet I still dare to hope when I remember this:*
> *The faithful love of the LORD never ends! His mercies never cease.*
> *Great is his faithfulness; his mercies begin afresh each morning.*
> *I say to myself, "The LORD is my inheritance; therefore, I will hope in him!"*
>
> —Lamentations 3:19–24 NLT

Jeremiah trusted God's promises. Despite harsh circumstances, he believed the Lord was faithful to His covenant oath to Abraham. He knew God is faithful even when we are faithless! The unwavering character of God was Jeremiah's basis for hope. Great is His faithfulness! This hope connects the grand narrative of the Bible.

Yesterday in our journey through Scripture, we looked at King David and how his life pointed forward to the ultimate Shepherd King, Jesus Christ. After his death, David was succeeded by his son Solomon, the man God chose to build the Temple in Jerusalem. During his reign, Israel enjoyed peace and prosperity. Yet after his death, turmoil ensued, and the nation was divided into two kingdoms.

The Northern Kingdom (Israel) consisted of ten tribes led by a series of wicked kings who proved unfaithful to Yahweh. They led the people into pagan idolatry. The sad lesson from their experience is that we become enslaved to that which we worship. Eventually, the Northern Kingdom was conquered by the Assyrians and expelled from the Promised Land in 722 BC.

The Southern Kingdom (Judah) experienced seasons of faithfulness under good kings who loved Yahweh and kept the covenant. Unfortunately, those seasons were quickly followed by evil kings who led the people into idolatry. In 586 BC, the Babylonians destroyed Jerusalem, demolished the glorious Temple, and deported the people as slaves to Babylon (see 2 Kings 25:9–12).

Over hundreds of years, as these sad events unfolded, God called His prophets to warn His people to repent. Repentance means to turn from sin and experience God's mercy. In some situations, the people did repent and experienced brief revivals. But time and time again, they broke the covenant, which ultimately led to their destruction (see Deut. 28:62–65).

While in Babylonian captivity, the prophets became voices of hope, reminding the exiled people of God's faithfulness. Prophets like Isaiah, Ezekiel, and Daniel declared that God was not finished with His people. Their prophetic messages offered hope for restoration of the land, a New Covenant that human sinfulness could not break, and foretold the Messiah, who would make all things new!

The Old Testament is filled with hundreds of messianic prophecies that served to identify the One to come as Israel's Savior. Here are just a few:

> The Messiah would be a descendant of King David
> —2 Samuel 7:12.
> The Messiah would be born in Bethlehem—Micah 5:2.
> The Messiah would be born of a virgin—Isaiah 7:14.
> The Messiah would be called God's Son—Psalm 2:1–12.
> The Messiah would usher in the New Covenant
> —Jeremiah 31:31–34.
> The Messiah would set captives free—Isaiah 61.
> The Messiah would be betrayed for thirty pieces of silver
> —Zechariah 11:12–13.
> The Messiah would enter Jerusalem riding on a donkey
> —Zechariah 9:9.
> The Messiah would suffer, die, and rise from the dead
> —Isaiah 53.
> The Messiah would be pierced—Zechariah 12:10.
> The Messiah would be resurrected—Psalm 16:8–11.

There were four hundred years of silence between the prophets who foretold of the Messiah and His birth in Bethlehem. During that time, God's people waited with expectation. Then, the day finally arrived for the One who perfectly fulfilled every promise to step from heaven to earth. Jesus understood He was the anticipated Messiah, and Luke's Gospel tells us, "Beginning with Moses and all the Prophets, he interpreted to them in all the Scriptures the things concerning himself" (24:27 ESV).

Oh, how I wish I could have sat in that Bible class when the disciples listened as Jesus explained His story from garden to garden, proving He was the long-awaited Redeemer! Although Jesus could not orchestrate the circumstances of His birth or the dramatic details of His death, He fully comprehended that His life and ministry fulfilled these promises.

Fulfilled prophecy provides dramatic evidence that the Bible is not simply a collection of stories, but the supernatural revelation of God's eternal plan of redemption. Nothing has fueled my faith more in seasons of waiting than to see how faithful the Lord is to keep His word. Friend, God's past faithfulness is an indicator of His future performance. The Lord has a proven track record. I'm learning that even when I can't see Him working, I can trust—"Great is his faithfulness" (Lam. 3:23 NLT).

Tomorrow, we turn the page to behold Emmanuel, God with us. Jesus' arrival as the long-awaited Messiah fulfilled the promise God spoke to Adam and Eve in the garden, the blessing promised to Abraham and his descendants, and the covenant made with King David of an eternal throne. These promises spoken to the prophets throughout the ages culminate in the One who is called the Word of God and made His home among us! (See John 1:14.) Although we could never return to God's Presence on our own, in His mercy, God came near. Our living hope is that heaven invaded earth in time and space history, and the One whom the saints of old longed to see arrived just as He was promised.

*Let us hold fast the confession of our hope without wavering, for he who promised is faithful.*

—Hebrews 10:23 ESV

## HARVEST

Are you familiar with the challenging or even painful process of waiting? What are you specifically waiting on God for in this season? Read the SEED passage (Jer. 29:11) again. Just as the prophets of the Old Testament had to trust the Lord in times of darkness, we, too, often find ourselves waiting for the dawn. Take some time to reflect on God's proven faithfulness in His Word and the ways you've seen Him provide in your own life. Ask Him to help you trust that He is working even when you can't see it.

# EMMANUEL

*All of this occurred to fulfill the Lord's message through his prophet:*
*"Look! The virgin will conceive a child! She will give birth to a son, and they will call him Immanuel, which means 'God is with us.'"*

—Matthew 1:22–23 NLT

DAY 16

# THE WORD

## SEED

*And the Word became flesh and dwelt among us, and we have seen his glory, glory as of the only Son from the Father, full of grace and truth.*

—John 1:14 ESV

## CULTIVATE

Read John 1:1–18; Colossians 1:15–20.

## FLOURISH

Since the moment Adam and Eve believed the Serpent's lie and hungered for independence, the plight of the human story has been one of a grueling alienation from God. While Satan's temptation seemed alluring, sin always lies with false promises of freedom and pompous boasts of autonomy. We traded life *with God* in Eden for an existence marked by aimlessness, emptiness, and shamefulness.

But God.

The Lord knew the devastating consequences of Adam and Eve's choice, and there in the garden, He promised to redeem us. Although He was under no obligation to come to our rescue, the Lord knew full well that the human soul was designed for connection with Him. It was to restore this divine connection that God the Father sent His Son, Jesus, to become one of us.

He was given the name Emmanuel, which means "God with us." Jesus Christ, the One who is fully God and fully man, entered our story to serve as the divine bridge between heaven and earth. The existence of the man Jesus of Nazareth as a historical figure is undebatable. But how one answers the question of His heavenly identity and divine authority proves the definition of saving faith. To that end, in this "Emmanuel" section, we aim to reveal Jesus as the One promised since the Garden of Eden as the Savior of the world.

The question before us today is this: *Who is Jesus?* Was He merely a good teacher, a great moral revolutionary, a prophet, or something more? To discover the answer, we will dive into the Gospel of John. John was a disciple of Jesus Christ who wrote an eyewitness account of Jesus' life and ministry. He marveled at Christ's miracles, absorbed His teachings, and watched in horror as Jesus was crucified. But most importantly, John beheld the resurrected Christ. He shared a meal with Him, touched His nail-scarred hands, and stood in awe as Jesus ascended to His throne in heaven. At the conclusion of his Gospel account, John wrote:

> *Now Jesus did many other signs in the presence of the disciples, which are not written in this book; but these are written so that you may believe that Jesus is the Christ, the Son of God, and that by believing you may have life in his name.*
>
> —John 20:30–31 ESV

John wrote the Gospel for one purpose—"that you may believe." Because what we conclude about this Man, Jesus, who turned the world upside down, is the key to eternal life. Believing in Christ is our access to Eden and the only way our fellowship with God is restored. With this vital truth in mind, let's look at the opening line of John's Gospel and how he answered the question—Who is Jesus?

> *In the beginning was the Word, and the Word was with God, and the Word was God.*
>
> —John 1:1 ESV

As we leave the Old Testament, we must keep in mind the sweeping changes that occurred at the time of the New Testament. So far in our journey from garden to garden, we've traced the history of the Hebrew people and how God worked through Abraham's descendants to reveal His plan of redemption. In the New Testament, we discover how God fulfilled those promises through His Son (a descendant of Abraham), but we find that the culture and language of the Bible have changed.

Jesus Christ stepped into human history when Israel was under Roman occupation. Centuries had passed since Jerusalem was destroyed and the Israelites were deported to Babylon. Eventually, the Lord brought Israel back to the Promised Land, but they remained under an occupying ruler. First, the Babylonians were overthrown by the Persians, then the Persians by the Greeks, and finally, the Roman Empire dominated the world. Although Israel remained a distinct people, they lived in a world governed by caesars, steeped in Roman idolatry, and infused with Greek philosophy. To understand John's eyewitness testimony, we must keep these historical changes in mind.

This brief history lesson brings us to John chapter 1 and one of the most profound revelations in the entire Bible. I say profound because John faced an impossible task: *How to explain the identity of Jesus Christ to two vastly different cultures.* As a Jewish man living in a Roman world, how did John explain the majestic messianic

King, who was a direct descendant from King David to a people unfamiliar with such promises? Under the inspiration of the Holy Spirit, John brilliantly chose a title that bridged these two worlds. That title was "Logos."

*Logos* is a Greek term that translates into English as "the Word" (see John 1:1–3). It means an expression of thought, an utterance, or a reason. For example, for you to know my private thoughts, I need to speak, write, or convey them to you. Otherwise, my intention or will is not understood. Therefore, John took this term, *logos*—common to both people—and applied it to Jesus. Jesus is the Word, the ultimate message and revelation of God to the world. We can know the Father's heart, mind, and will because He speaks through His Son, Jesus.

To further understand how John identifies Jesus, we need to dig a little more into the ancient Greek culture. *Logos* was commonly used by Greek philosophers who attempted to answer life's big questions: *Who are we? Why are we here? What is the meaning of life?* Through debating these hefty philosophical questions, they wanted to discover the "Ultimate Reality"—the divine reason behind all things. They pondered:

Why does this world exist?
How did it come into existence?
What purpose does it hold?

Over time, the term *Logos* became synonymous with "Ultimate Reality." Therefore, when John penned his Gospel, he intentionally chose "Logos" as the primary way to answer the question—Who is Jesus? He is the Ultimate Reality. He is the Creator of all things. He is the reason all things exist—the invisible power behind the universe.

But let's not forget that John was a Jewish man who also wrote to Hebrew people. For the Jews, there was no mystery concerning Ultimate Reality; they believed in Elohim, the Creator, who brought forth all life by speaking the universe into existence. For a Jewish person, the opening line of John's Gospel—"In the beginning was the Word" (ESV)—would immediately recall the very first words of Genesis: "In the beginning God created the heavens and the earth" (Gen. 1:1 NIV). The connection is clear: The One John calls "the Word" is Elohim! From that dramatic introduction, John goes on to declare that the Word—the Ultimate Reality—became one of us.

> *And the Word became flesh and dwelt among us, and we have seen his glory, glory as of the only Son from the Father, full of grace and truth.*
>
> —John 1:14 ESV

John said, "We have seen his glory" with our own eyes. This is John's eyewitness testimony. For a Jewish man, that was not just a nice way of saying Jesus did miraculous things. John is referring to the resplendent Shekinah glory of God! This is the Presence of Yahweh that Moses encountered at the burning bush, the glory that led God's people in a cloud by day and in a fire by night through the wilderness, and the awesome Presence that filled the Holy of Holies in the Temple. John declares that the Shekinah glory of God took up residence in Jesus Christ and moved into our neighborhood! Let that truth just boggle your mind for a minute!

> *Long ago, at many times and in many ways, God spoke to our fathers by the prophets, but in these last days he has spoken to us by his Son, whom he appointed the heir of all things,*

*through whom also he created the world. He is the radiance of the glory of God and the exact imprint of his nature, and he upholds the universe by the word of his power.*

—Hebrews 1:1–3 ESV

## HARVEST

Ponder the SEED passage, John 1:14. Now that you have a deeper understanding of what John was conveying by calling Jesus "the Word," does that change how you understand who Jesus is? What does it mean to you that "the Word became flesh and dwelt among us"?

DAY 17

# THE SON OF MAN

## SEED

*No one has ascended into heaven except he who descended from heaven, the Son of Man.*

—John 3:13 ESV

## CULTIVATE

Read John 3:1–21; Daniel 7:9–14.

## FLOURISH

When many people think of Christmas, images of Hallmark movies, snow-clad tree farms, mistletoe, twinkling lights, Santa Claus, and candy canes fill their minds. Of course, I am game for all the fun holiday traditions; truthfully, I have watched my fair share of holiday chick flicks. But I think a sappy movie about high school sweethearts reuniting is a far cry from what the birth of Jesus is actually about.

The advent of Jesus was a cataclysmic event that dawned a new era. As I look at the whole scope of redemptive history, I find the incarnation much more like the D-Day invasion than a romantic comedy reunion. D-Day was the strategic move by the Allied forces that changed the course of history and brought about the defeat of Nazi Germany during World War II. Under Hitler's reign, Nazi forces gobbled up nations and terrorized the Western world. That is until June 6, 1941, when Allied forces landed on the shores of Normandy in France. This invasion gained a foothold against the enemy, ultimately pushing them back to Berlin, where they were eventually defeated.

I liken Jesus' birth to a military invasion because it marked when Jesus stepped from His throne in heaven and entered enemy-occupied territory. Robed in humanity, He was born a babe in Bethlehem. After living in obscurity, He began His public ministry, then endured the long march toward the cross, where He defeated Satan and his kingdom. The apostle Paul used a similar metaphor to describe the ministry of Jesus:

> *He has delivered us from the domain of darkness and transferred us to the kingdom of his beloved Son.*
>
> —Colossians 1:13 ESV

Make no mistake, Jesus is the long-awaited "Seed of the woman" who came from heaven to earth to vanquish the Enemy and release those captive to his schemes.

There are many titles given to Jesus throughout the Bible. But the one He most often employed was Son of Man. He used this messianic title because it identified Him as the promised "Seed of the woman" and affirmed His humanity. As C. S. Lewis famously said in *Mere Christianity*, "The Son of God became a man to enable men to become sons of God."[1] But there's more to this title that bears exploring.

In the Old Testament, a godly man named Daniel received visions from the Lord about the Messiah who would usher in the Kingdom of God. In one such vision, Daniel saw heaven and the

---

1 Lewis, *Mere Christianity*, 155.

Ancient of Days (God the Father) seated upon His throne. Next, Daniel saw another figure—the Son of Man.

> *I saw in the night visions,*
> *and behold, with the clouds of heaven*
> *there came one like a son of man,*
> *and he came to the Ancient of Days*
> *and was presented before him.*
> *And to him was given dominion*
> *and glory and a kingdom,*
> *that all peoples, nations, and languages*
> *should serve him;*
> *his dominion is an everlasting dominion,*
> *which shall not pass away,*
> *and his kingdom one*
> *that shall not be destroyed.*
>
> —Daniel 7:13–14 ESV

This prophetic vision shows the Son of Man given authority, glory, sovereign power, dominion, and an eternal kingdom—the Kingdom of God. Why does this matter? Because God's redemptive plan that was promised in the Garden of Eden was unfolding before Daniel's eyes! What Adam lost in the Garden of Eden would be restored by One called the Son of Man. In the garden, Adam lost the right to rule over the earth (dominion), he lost authority, and he fell from glory. But in the Son of Man's Kingdom, the curse is reversed!

This prophetic vision brings us back to the New Testament and the Gospel of John. When Jesus entered His public ministry, He came proclaiming the Kingdom of God and called Himself "the Son of Man." His miracles validated He was the Messiah as

He exercised dominion over the natural realm, authority over demons, and sovereignty over sickness.

This background leads us to John chapter 3, where Jesus met with Nicodemus under the cloak of darkness and talked about the Kingdom of God. Nicodemus said, "Rabbi, we know that you are a teacher come from God, for no one can do these signs that you do unless God is with him" (John 3:2 ESV).

Nicodemus was aware of the miracles Jesus performed, such as turning water into wine, casting out demons, and healing the sick. He rightly recognized that those would be impossible without God's power and authority. Jesus replied, "Truly, truly, I say to you, unless one is born again he cannot see the kingdom of God" (John 3:3 ESV).

As a prominent religious man, Nicodemus was aware of the messianic prophecies and familiar with the promises of the Kingdom. He wanted to know *how* to enter it. Jesus' instructions that he must be "born again" greatly perplexed him. Naturally, he wanted to know, "How is this even possible?"—in response to which Jesus shared the secret to entering the Kingdom of God: faith in the Son of Man.

> *No one has ascended into heaven except he who descended from heaven, the Son of Man. And as Moses lifted up the serpent in the wilderness, so must the Son of Man be lifted up, that whoever believes in him may have eternal life.*
>
> —John 3:13–15 ESV

Jesus used a pivotal moment in Israel's history to explain how one enters the Kingdom of God. First, Jesus reminded Nicodemus of when the children of Israel were in the wilderness. Due to a rebellion, a great horde of snakes attacked them. In the midst of their suffering, the Lord told Moses how they could be saved from the snake venom.

The prescription was to lift high a bronze serpent, and all who looked up to the bronze serpent would be healed of their affliction. Jesus used this perplexing illustration to explain His ministry as the Son of Man. Just as the bronze serpent was lifted up to cure the effects of the snake venom, so He would be lifted high on a cross to cure our sin problem. Here's the Gospel truth: Anyone who by faith looks to Him on the cross is saved from the poison of sin and given eternal life.

But why did God do this? Why did God the Father send Jesus as the Son of Man to take away the venom that courses through our veins? The invasion of heaven to earth proves the most ultimate display of love this world has ever known. Jesus answered the question of "Why?" with what has become the most famous verse in the Bible. Let these familiar words envelop you as you imagine the depth of love that God poured out for you by sending His Son to invade enemy-occupied territory in order to rescue you.

> *For God so loved the world, that he gave his only Son, that whoever believes in him should not perish but have eternal life. For God did not send his Son into the world to condemn the world, but in order that the world might be saved through him.*
>
> —John 3:16–17 ESV

## HARVEST

Perhaps you have heard John 3:16 many times, and you may even have it committed to memory. Or, maybe it's the first time you've really understood these famous words of Jesus. Take a minute to carefully meditate on it as if you've never read it before. What words or key phrases stand out? Let this sink deep into your heart: God sent His Son because He loves YOU. He wanted to rescue YOU. And then read 3:17 again. How does it resonate with you that Jesus said He came *not to condemn* the world, but *to rescue* it?

## DAY 18

# THE MIRACLES

### SEED

*This miraculous sign at Cana in Galilee was the first time Jesus revealed his glory. And his disciples believed in him.*

—John 2:11 NLT

### CULTIVATE

Read John 2; Ephesians 3:20–21.

### FLOURISH

A miracle is an extraordinary event inexplicable by natural or scientific laws and considered a work of a divine agency. I love a good miracle story. Nothing gets me more pumped than reading a Bible story or hearing a testimony about God showing up and showing off!

Miracles are moments when the power of heaven pierces earth.

Miracles are the fingerprints of God on the pages of history.

Miracles reveal who is in charge and the "divine agency" of the One who truly calls the shots.

Miracles provide evidence that there is another dimension beyond what we see with our eyes.

Jesus stepped into human history to redeem us from sin and to restore our fellowship with God the Father. As Randy Alcorn rightly observes, "Jesus' miracles provide us with a sample of the meaning of redemption: a freeing of creation from the shackles of sin and evil and a reinstatement of creaturely living as intended by God."[1] He came announcing the arrival of the Kingdom of God and that access to it was available through faith in Him.

Now it's one thing for Jesus to announce the Kingdom but quite another thing for Him to reveal it (see Luke 17:21). Pastor Tim Keller explains how Christ's supernatural acts revealed His Kingdom and pointed toward a return to Eden:

> We modern people think of miracles as the suspension of the natural order, but Jesus meant them to be the restoration of the natural order. The Bible tells us that God did not originally make the world to have disease, hunger, and death in it. Jesus has come to redeem where it is wrong and heal the world where it is broken. His miracles are not just proofs that he has power but also wonderful foretastes of what he is going to do with that power. Jesus' miracles are not just a challenge to our minds, but a promise to our hearts, that the world we all want is coming.[2]

Whether it was giving sight to a blind man, walking on water, multiplying food to feed thousands, healing a leper, or raising the dead—His miracles served to validate that He was the long-awaited Messiah, sent from heaven to earth. Jesus' miracles were supernatural acts that signified His identity and mission. One specific Old Testament prophecy predicted that the Messiah would work miracles:

---

1 Alcorn, *Heaven*, 89.

2 Tim Keller, *The Reason for God: Belief in an Age of Skepticism* (New York: Dutton, 2008), 95.

*Then the eyes of the blind shall be opened,*
*and the ears of the deaf unstopped;*
*then shall the lame man leap like a deer,*
*and the tongue of the mute sing for joy.*
*For waters break forth in the wilderness,*
*and streams in the desert.*

—Isaiah 35:5–6 ESV

All four Gospels record various ways Jesus revealed His heavenly power. In fact, Jesus performed so many miracles that John, who penned the Gospel that bears his name, said: "Now there are also many other things that Jesus did. Were every one of them to be written, I suppose that the world itself could not contain the books that would be written" (John 21:25 ESV).

Randy Alcorn states:

> The Bible shows that in His unfolding drama of redemption, God is at work to reclaim not just our souls, but also our bodies, and not just our bodies, but also the earth from which that first human body was made, and over which God purposed us to reign.[3]

John beheld so many wondrous episodes that he thought it impossible to record them all. Instead, under the inspiration of the Holy Spirit, John narrowed down his eyewitness account to seven specific events that revealed that Jesus was indeed the "Divine Agent" ruling the world. The seven signs in the Gospel of John serve as a billboard that declares Jesus is God with us!

---

3 Randy Alcorn, "Albert Wolters's Creation Regained, and the Vast Redemptive Scope of the Gospel," https://www.epm.org/blog/2022/Jun/10/creation-regained.

The first miracle occurred at a wedding in Cana (see John 2). The details are sparse, but we do know that Jesus arrived at a wedding, bringing His disciple with Him. Before we get into the nature of this supernatural event, a little background on Jewish culture will help us appreciate the symbolism behind it.

During biblical times, Jewish weddings were a big deal. But, for a culture that prided itself on hospitality, weddings took it to a whole other level. Hebrew engagements extended over a year and culminated in a wedding feast that usually lasted a week. The wedding feast was a celebration in which the groom hosted all their friends, families, and neighbors for days of eating, drinking, and joyful celebration.

At some point in this particular wedding feast, the groom's family ran out of wine, which would have brought tremendous shame upon them. While we don't know the connection, we know that Mary, the mother of Jesus, was intimate with the family and learned of the situation. Mary told Jesus, and the text infers that she wanted Him to solve the social blunder.

Jesus responded by saying, "My time has not yet come" (John 2:4 NLT). Jesus grasped the prophetic significance of performing a miracle. He knew the minute He revealed His glory that the national spotlight would turn on Him and bring Israel's messianic hopes with it.

By all accounts, the miracle was simple. The Master of Molecules turned water into wine. But how did this transformation take place? We aren't given any special words or phrases, just a command given to the servants. Jesus told the servants to take the stone water jars meant for religious purification and fill them to the rim. The servants obeyed, and as they dipped the cups into the pitchers, they saw the evidence before their eyes—the water had turned into wine! Not just any wine, but according to the head waiter, this was the finest wine!

Here's the question we must ask ourselves: Of all the thousands of miracles that John witnessed Jesus perform, why did he share this one? Each of the miracles in John's Gospel is a sign that validates Jesus' identity. But this specific miracle powerfully visualized the New Covenant.

Recall that the Old Covenant was written by God on tablets of stone and given to Moses on Mount Sinai. The Mosaic covenant was conditional and depended upon God's people keeping the Law. As we've seen through our survey of the Old Testament, they continually rebelled and turned away from Yahweh. As a result, they became captives to other nations. Time and time again, God raised up the prophets, who promised a Messiah who would deliver His people from their sinful ways and bring a New Covenant, which by God's grace would no longer be written on tablets of stone but on the human heart.

This miracle symbolizes the transformation that occurs in the human heart. Under the Old Covenant, the water jars were used for purification rituals, during which the people continually washed their hands and eating utensils in an attempt to achieve purity. But as we've seen, cleaning the outside didn't change the nature of the human heart. The human heart needs a miracle—a touch of grace!

Jesus transformed the water into wine. This was a picture of redemption. In Christ, we are transformed. God takes away our hearts of stone and gives us new hearts, filled with His love, joy, and peace. Transforming water into wine symbolized the supernatural miracle that happens in the human heart when we come to Christ.

While we continue to survey the Bible from garden to garden, we can't help but pause and marvel at the wink from heaven revealed in this miracle. Friend, God is in the details. The Bible begins with a wedding in the Garden of Eden and concludes with a wedding at the end of Revelation. How fitting then that Jesus, the One sent from heaven to earth as our Redeemer, launched His public ministry with a miraculous sign at a wedding. After all, the heart of the wedding is a covenant through which two people become one. This mingling of souls that we call the marriage covenant is the very reason the Son of God entered our human story. So that through the miracle of God's transforming grace, we could once again become one with Him.

> *Therefore, if anyone is in Christ, he is a new creation; old things have passed away; behold, all things have become new.*
>
> —2 Corinthians 5:17 NKJV

## HARVEST

Today we pondered the miraculous signs performed by Jesus that proved He was the long-awaited Messiah. Turning water into wine symbolized the ultimate transformation in the human heart. Think about your own life. Can others see the power of God at work in transforming you? How have you been changed by Jesus? Take a minute to talk to the Lord about any area or struggle that needs the power of His transforming grace.

## DAY 19

# THE LIVING WATER

### SEED

*Jesus said to her, "Everyone who drinks of this water will be thirsty again, but whoever drinks of the water that I will give him will never be thirsty again. The water that I will give him will become in him a spring of water welling up to eternal life."*

—John 4:13–14 ESV

### CULTIVATE

Read John 4:1–42; Psalm 107.

### FLOURISH

When was the last time you were truly thirsty? Take a second and remember that feeling. The symptoms of dehydration are easy to identify—cracked lips, sunken eyes, and dry skin. Dehydration is a dangerous state because our bodies can live only a few days without water before our internal organs begin to shut down. But the reality is there are two kinds of thirst: physical and spiritual. Spiritual dehydration manifests in our insecurities, addictive behavior, chronic need for approval, and an emptiness that can't be filled by any substance, person, accolade, possession, or experience.

The Bible speaks of this condition: "I thirst for God, the living God. When can I go and stand before him?" (Ps. 42:2 NLT). Why are we spiritually dehydrated? That problem takes us all the way back to the Garden of Eden. We were made by God and for a relationship with Him, but the human condition has been a vain attempt to fill our souls with a substitute ever since.

C. S. Lewis advises,

> God made us: invented us as a man invents an engine. A car is made to run on petrol, and it would not properly on anything else. Now God designed the human machine to run on Himself.[1]

This is the beauty of the redemption story. Not only did Jesus come as the Messiah to forgive our sin problem, but He came to quench our deepest thirst. In John 4, we find Jesus intentionally charting His course to bring Living Water to a woman suffering from spiritual dehydration.

Jesus was traveling from Judea to Galilee. Without trains, planes, or automobiles, this meant a multiple-day walk in an arid environment. Without the modern luxuries we employ when hiking, Jesus relied on natural streams and wells to provide the water His body needed. After traveling for several days, the Middle Eastern sun scorched the sky when Jesus finally arrived in Samaria.

For Jesus to even be in this region was unusual for a Jewish man. The Israelites scorned the Samaritans and considered them unclean. Their prejudice stemmed from racial and religious differences. Pious Jews went out of their way to avoid the area, fearful of being guilty by association.

---

1 Lewis, *Mere Christianity*, bk. 2, chap. 3, "The Shocking Alternative."

Jesus deliberately traveled through this notorious neighborhood because He knew a divine appointment awaited Him. As Jesus sat by the well, a nameless woman came at noon to fetch water. She, too, was tired. Not just from carrying her empty water jar, but from lugging the weight of her empty heart. The story's context tells us that she was an outcast in her society because of her checkered past. As she tentatively approached the well, Jesus said, "Give me a drink" (John 4:7 ESV). Puzzled by the cultural taboos he was breaking, she asked, "How is it that you, a Jew, ask for a drink from me, a woman of Samaria?" (4:9 ESV). In that day, men did not speak to women in public, nor did Jews talk to Samaritans.

Ignoring her objections, Jesus said, "If you knew the gift of God, and who it is that is saying to you, 'Give me a drink,' you would have asked him, and he would have given you living water" (John 4:10 ESV). Intrigued, she wanted to know more. Jesus explained that He offered something better—a gift that could never be found in any earthly river, stream, or well.

> *Jesus said to her, "Everyone who drinks of this water will be thirsty again, but whoever drinks of the water that I will give him will never be thirsty again. The water that I will give him will become in him a spring of water welling up to eternal life." The woman said to him, "Sir, give me this water, so that I will not be thirsty or have to come here to draw water."*
>
> —John 4:13–15 ESV

Of course, she wanted to never thirst again! Now that He had her attention, Jesus turned the conversation to the real issue—her soul's deep thirst for God. He asked her to go get her husband. She responded that she didn't have a husband. At this Jesus revealed He knew her story:

> *The woman answered him, "I have no husband." Jesus said to her, "You are right in saying, 'I have no husband'; for you have had five husbands, and the one you now have is not your husband. What you have said is true."*
>
> —John 4:17–18 ESV

Five husbands? I imagine her journey from marriage to marriage—each time with a glimmer of hope that perhaps this time she would finally find the love her soul craved. My heart breaks for the disappointment she must have felt and the sheer disillusionment that settled in after each relationship ended without satisfying her deep ache for love.

A. W. Tozer explains:

> In the deep heart of the man was a shrine where none but God was worthy to come. Within him was God, without, a thousand gifts which God had showered upon him. But sin introduced complications and has made those very gifts of God a potential source of ruin to the soul. Our woes began when God was forced out of His central shrine and "things" were allowed to enter...God's gifts now take the place of God, and the whole course of nature is upset by the monstrous substitution.[2]

Jesus diagnosed her spiritual condition and how she had attempted to quench her thirst for love with men. He didn't reveal her situation to shame her but to free her from the endless cycle of looking for love in all the wrong places. Once she realized Jesus knew her story, she assumed He was a prophet.

To deflect from the real issue, she changed the subject to a hotly

---

2 Tozer, *Pursuit of God*, 21–22.

contested religious question: What was the proper place to worship God? Jesus was not derailed by this distraction and explained that true worship is not about meeting in a physical location but about the state of our hearts.

How perfectly ironic! Here was a nameless woman who searched for man after man to fill her emptiness, and the Author of Life sat before her offering what her soul needed most—the unconditional love of God.

> *The woman said, "I know the Messiah is coming—the one who is called Christ. When he comes, he will explain everything to us." Then Jesus told her, "I AM the Messiah!"*
>
> —John 4:25–26 NLT

Imagine hearing Jesus declare, "I am the Messiah!" Since the Garden of Eden, humanity has longed for the arrival of the Redeemer, and of all the people Jesus could reveal His identity to, He chose this woman. Rather than notifying the religious leaders, Jesus pursued a woman who needed to know God saw her, loved her, and wanted to give her the gift of eternal life.

After her encounter with Christ, the woman returned to her village to tell everyone that she had met the Messiah! Her testimony was simple: Jesus knew everything about her and still loved her! In her haste, she left behind her empty water jar, which perfectly symbolizes the transformation that happened in her soul. Leaving the shame and emptiness of her past behind, she was now filled to the brim with God's love and ready to tell anyone who would listen about the Living Water!

I can easily empathize with the woman at the well and her chronic state of spiritual dehydration. I know her desperation all too well. That was my life before Jesus. I, too, searched for a soul-filling love in all the wrong places: continually running from man to man and bottle to bottle to find the security and acceptance that can be found only in a real relationship with God.

Like the woman at the well, I finally came to see the emptiness of my life and discovered that only God can fill the God-shaped hole in our souls. Thankfully, the One who introduced Himself as the Living Water is the same God who pursues us, redeems us, and truly satisfies our souls with a river of abundant life.

> *For he satisfies the longing soul,*
> *and the hungry soul he fills with good things.*
>
> —Psalm 107:9 ESV

## HARVEST

Friend, is your soul longing for something that only God can truly satisfy? If you are feeling empty today, set aside the distractions you might normally reach for to fill you. Be honest with God; where are you tempted to look for life and satisfaction other than Him? Instead, turn your hungry soul to the only One who can fill it with "good things" and ask Him to fill your heart and soul with His life, love, and power.

## DAY 20

# THE PLOT THICKENS

### SEED

*Jesus answered, "I tell you the truth, before Abraham was even born, I AM!" At that point they picked up stones to throw at him. But Jesus was hidden from them and left the Temple.*

—John 8:58–59 NLT

### CULTIVATE

Read John 8; Psalm 2.

### FLOURISH

The life and ministry of Jesus are revealed in the Bible through four Gospels: Matthew, Mark, Luke, and John. Each Gospel serves a unique purpose, but it is in John's Gospel that we see most clearly that Jesus is not just a Man; He is Emmanuel, God with us.

It was Jesus' claim to equality with God that riled the religious leaders of His day and ultimately caused them to plot His crucifixion. But make no mistake, Jesus was no martyr. He knew precisely who He was and what His mission was on earth. Therefore, as we continue to survey Scripture from garden to garden and behold Emmanuel, we don't find Jesus stepping away from conflict; rather, we see Him confronting religious hypocrisy, standing for truth, and declaring unashamedly that He is the heaven-sent Son of God.

The context for Jesus' claim to divinity is an event found in John 8:1–11. Here we find Jesus at the center of a drama involving the religious leaders and an unnamed woman. Jesus was teaching in the Temple courts when chaos erupted as Israel's religious leaders brought in a woman whom they caught in adultery. We must remove our modern lenses for a minute to fully appreciate the weightiness of this situation. In that culture, this sinful act could have been a death sentence for this woman.

I imagine she sobbed and quaked in fear as the others screamed accusations and threw her at Jesus' feet. The irony of this scene is that it was Jesus who was actually on trial by the religious authorities; the woman merely served as a pawn in their game.

A little background into this text will help us understand what this confrontation was all about. The religious leaders were jealous of Jesus' popularity and threatened by this man who gave sight to the blind, healed lepers, and enabled the lame to walk. Not only that, but His teachings also challenged their spiritual authority, and His miracles validated His claims. As a result, a plot formed among the various religious leaders to discredit and get rid of Jesus.

We do not know whether they intentionally set up the adulterous rendezvous or just learned of the affair. John 8 says she was caught in the act, and her marital unfaithfulness was a death sentence at that time. They tossed her in front of Jesus and lobbed their accusation at Him: This woman was caught in the act of adultery, and the law of Moses demanded that she be stoned to death. Then they asked the trick question: "What do you say?" (John 8:5 NLT).

They assumed they had Jesus cornered. I imagine they smirked in triumph and reasoned: "If He ignores the Law and shows her mercy, we could use that to discredit Him." But Jesus saw through the charade, and rather than debating, He stooped to the ground and wrote. Bible scholars have long debated what Jesus wrote. Whatever He scribbled in the dirt silenced the condemning mob. Some think He wrote the Ten Commandments. Others believe He listed the secret sins of her accusers. Either way, when He finished, Jesus stood up and looked in their eyes and said, "Let him who is without sin among you be the first to throw a stone at her" (John 8:7 ESV).

Brilliant! Jesus turned the tables on them, and now the accusers had to ask themselves some questions.

*Am I without sin?*

*Can I stand in judgment of another?*

*Does my righteousness measure up to the law of God?*

The only person who could pass the righteousness test and throw a stone at that woman was the One standing between her and her accusers. The only sinless person who ever lived is Jesus Christ. He challenged her condemners to examine their own hearts. Upon hearing Jesus' declaration, the men dropped their stones and walked away. Why? Because they recognized their own sinfulness. God's law is like a mirror, revealing our hearts and our desperate need for God's grace. As a result, one by one, her accusers turned away and dropped their stones at Jesus' feet.

Jesus looked at the woman and said: "'Woman, where are they? Has no one condemned you?' She said, 'No one, Lord.' And Jesus said, 'Neither do I condemn you; go, and from now on sin no more'" (John 8:10–11 ESV).

Let's be clear: Jesus did not condone adultery with a wink and a smile. Although He didn't condemn her, He called her to repentance by saying: "Go now and leave your life of sin." Jesus honored the sacredness of the marriage covenant. At the same time, He saw through the hypocrisy of her accusers and exposed their judgmental hearts. Pastor Tim Keller perfectly describes Jesus' response:

> Jesus did not come with a sword in his hands; he came with nails in his hands. He did not come to bring judgment; he came to bear judgment.[1]

The very reason Jesus came from heaven to earth was to bear the punishment that each of us deserves for our sin. That is why we call Him Savior. He comes to the rescue of those who recognize their need for Him.

This story doesn't end with the religious leaders skulking away. These same men picked up stones again, but the next time, Jesus would be their target. The next day, Jesus engaged in a lengthy debate with the religious authorities. Frustrated that they were unable to discredit Jesus the previous day, they came back again and pestered Him with questions about His identity, authority, and right to pronounce forgiveness of sins. Round after round, Jesus stood His ground and declared that His identity and power came from heaven (see John 8:12–59).

Frustrated by Jesus' unwillingness to back down, the leaders called Him names, accused Him of being demon-possessed, and even suggested that He was an illegitimate child. This led to the statement that sealed Jesus' fate when the debate turned to the subject of Abraham, the father of the Hebrew people.

The religious leaders placed their hope on being descendants of Abraham. Jesus reminded them of the true nature of the covenant and how Abraham looked forward to Jesus' day, when the promise of a worldwide blessing would be realized. They scoffed at this and

---

1 Tim Keller, *Encounters with Jesus: Unexpected Answers to Life's Biggest Questions* (New York: Penguin, 2015), 54.

reminded Jesus of His age and how impossible it was for Abraham to know Him. To this, Jesus said:

> *I tell you the truth, before Abraham was even born, I AM!*
>
> —John 8:58 NLT

Don't miss this. Jesus evoked the holy covenant name of God as His own. Scripture tells us that those men immediately picked up stones to kill Jesus for such a claim. Make no mistake, the Jewish leaders knew exactly what Jesus was claiming. When He said, "*I AM!*," He used the holy, sacred, covenant name of God as His own! Jesus dropped the mic, and the men picked up their stones. This was a clear claim of deity.

We can't underestimate the force of His words—Jesus identified Himself as Yahweh, the self-existent Lord God Almighty. The One who spoke to Moses from the burning bush, who redeemed His people from Egypt, and whose Shekinah glory dwelled in the Temple. I absolutely love how C. S. Lewis highlights the significance of this claim:

> I am trying here to prevent anyone saying the really foolish thing that people often say about Him: I'm ready to accept Jesus as a great moral teacher, but I don't accept his claim to be God. That is the one thing we must not say. A man who was merely a man and said the sort of things Jesus said would not be a great moral teacher. He would either be a lunatic—on the level with the man who says he is a poached egg—or else he would be the Devil of Hell. You must make your choice. Either this man was, and is, the Son of God, or else a madman or something worse. You can shut him up for a fool, you can spit at him and kill him as a demon or

> you can fall at his feet and call him Lord and God, but let us not come with any patronizing nonsense about his being a great human teacher. He has not left that open to us. He did not intend to.[2]

Because of Jesus' audacious claim, the religious leaders attempted to stone Him, and is it possible that they picked up the same stones they'd dropped the day before when He exposed their sinful hearts? Although John tells us that Jesus escaped from their trap, this moment sealed His destiny. His words were blasphemous in their eyes. And indeed, they would have been, except that they were true! Jesus had every right to evoke the holy name of God, because He is Emmanuel—God with us. Although Jesus slipped away that day, it was this dramatic confrontation that set the chain of events in motion that led to His crucifixion.

> *For in Christ lives all the fullness of God in a human body.*
>
> —Colossians 2:9 NLT

## HARVEST

As noted above, C. S. Lewis famously quipped that Jesus was either a liar, a lunatic, or we must "fall at his feet and call him Lord." Based on what you've discovered so far about Jesus Christ, why is this statement true? Would a mere man do and say the things that Jesus did? If Jesus is truly God with us, how does that change how you respond to Him? Take time to process the reality of His Lordship.

---

2 Lewis, *Mere Christianity*, 52.

DAY 21

# THE HOPE OF ETERNAL LIFE

## SEED

*Jesus said to her, "I am the resurrection and the life. Whoever believes in me, though he die, yet shall he live."*

—John 11:25 ESV

## CULTIVATE

Read John 11–12.

## FLOURISH

My beloved mother-in-law passed away two summers ago after a ten-year battle with breast cancer. We are so thankful that she outlived her prognosis by many years. Round after round of chemo, clinical trials, and radiation, and not once did I hear her complain. She consistently thought of others during her battle. I've never known a tougher woman in my life. Although she fought hard, in the end, the horrific illness took its toll.

We sat by her bed as she entered the final stages. The weeks of hospice care are a blur; I mostly remember watching my husband grieve with tears streaming down his face. No words describe the anguish of those days. I imagine that most of you can relate in some way. Death is an unwelcome guest that visits us all.

Through those long years of praying for healing and hoping for a cure, one aspect of our faith came into the forefront—the hope of eternal life. Death doesn't get the final say. Cancer is not the winner in this story. Jesus' promise of resurrection life echoed through my heart during the hardest of days.

Since sin entered the world in the Garden of Eden, the curse of death has reigned over humanity. Satan lied to Eve when he hissed, "You will not surely die" (Gen. 3:4 ESV). From battlefields to hospital beds, the truth is known, and we've longed for a Redeemer to rescue us from the ultimate enemy. After centuries of waiting and watching, praying and hoping, the One who came to conquer sin and death (the promised "Seed of the woman") stepped into the human story. Jesus clothed Himself in our mortality—He became one of us in order to redeem us.

In our SEED focal passage today, we hear Jesus make an audacious claim. His words, along with the other "I AM" statements recorded in the Gospel of John, were clear claims of divinity and descriptive of His ministry.

To the spiritually hungry, He is the Bread of Life.
To those lost in darkness, He is the Light of the World.
To the thirsty, He is the Living Water.
To those trying to find their way home, He is the Way, the Truth, and the Life.
To the one beaten down by the Enemy, He is the Good Shepherd.
To those facing the reality of death, He is the Resurrection and the Life!

Each of the "I AM" statements of Christ revealed who Jesus is and what He came to accomplish. This proves especially true in His claim, "I am the Resurrection and the Life!"

In John 11 Jesus confronts our greatest enemy and reveals His power to reverse the curse of death. As an eyewitness to this miracle, John tells us that although Jesus learned that His friend Lazarus was ill, He didn't immediately rush to heal the sickness. Days later, Jesus traveled to Lazarus's home in Bethany, where He was met by two sisters—Martha and Mary. Lazarus's sisters loved Jesus and were greatly disappointed that He didn't step in and stop their brother from dying (see John 11:1–21).

By the time Jesus arrived, Lazarus had been in the tomb for four days. These details are given to reveal the magnitude of this miracle. Healing the sick is one thing but raising a dead man to life is on a whole other level! Jesus was first greeted by Martha, and their conversation provides one of the greatest revelations by Jesus of His mission.

> *Jesus said to her, "Your brother will rise again." Martha said to him, "I know that he will rise again in the resurrection on the last day." Jesus said to her, "I am the resurrection and the life. Whoever believes in me, though he die, yet shall he live, and everyone who lives and believes in me shall never die. Do you believe this?"*
>
> —John 11:23–26 ESV

Not only did John convey the miraculous moments in Jesus' life, but thankfully, he also shared the tender, kind, and compassionate tidbits as well. For in John 11:35, we find the shortest verse in the entire Bible—"Jesus wept" (ESV). These two words drip with

God's heart for the brokenness of our world. God created us for life; therefore, when Jesus stood before His friend's tomb, He wept over the senseless loss and suffering.

Wiping away His tears, Jesus stepped forward and reversed the curse. At first the sisters protested; they knew the body was decomposing and told Jesus that it was too late. But there is no such thing as "too late" with Jesus—He is always right on time. The Lord commanded death to release him and said, "Lazarus, come out" (John 11:43 ESV). Saint Augustine once said that if Jesus had not said Lazarus's name, all the graves in the world would have opened! Instead, Lazarus stepped out of the tomb, still wrapped in graveclothes. I love how *The Expositor's Bible Commentary* explains this miracle:

> The creative power of God reversed the process of corruption and quickened the corpse into life. The effect was startling... it was a supreme demonstration of the power of eternal life that triumphed over death, corruption, and hopelessness.[1]

Don't miss that last line—the power of eternal life triumphed over hopelessness! The reason Christ-followers can grieve with hope is because death is not the end; we carry the promise of eternal life in Jesus!

After witnessing such a miracle, one would expect the masses to fall at Jesus' feet and worship Him. But, alas, that's not what happened. While many believed, others chose to harden their hearts. Although they couldn't deny the wondrous work, the religious leaders were more concerned with losing their power than what this miracle said about Jesus. The leaders conspired together,

---

1 M. C. Tenney, *John*, in F. E. Gaebelein, ed., *The Expositor's Bible Commentary: John and Acts* (Grand Rapids, MI: Zondervan, 1981), vol. 9, p. 121.

and John tells us that this event led to Jesus' crucifixion (see John 11:45–53).

What they didn't realize was that God would take their sinful motives and use them for good. It would be through Jesus' death that death would be defeated. The cross seemed like a victory for the Enemy, but it was the very means by which the "Seed of the woman" crushed his head!

Lazarus is a picture of all of us who put our faith in Jesus Christ. While we will face physical death, it is not the end of the story. Jesus wins! We will rise again! We have the hope of eternal life in Christ. The promise we cling to in this sin-stained world is that Christ triumphed over death on the cross! Victory is in Jesus—the Resurrection and the Life!

*Behold! I tell you a mystery. We shall not all sleep, but we shall all be changed, in a moment, in the twinkling of an eye, at the last trumpet. For the trumpet will sound, and the dead will be raised imperishable, and we shall be changed. For this perishable body must put on the imperishable, and this mortal body must put on immortality. When the perishable puts on the imperishable, and the mortal puts on immortality, then shall come to pass the saying that is written:*
*"Death is swallowed up in victory."*
*"O death, where is your victory?*
*O death, where is your sting?"*
*The sting of death is sin, and the power of sin is the law. But thanks be to God, who gives us the victory through our Lord Jesus Christ.*

—1 Corinthians 15:51–57 ESV

## HARVEST

Today we read several "I AM" statements that convey who Jesus is and why He came. Read again each of these statements, beginning with "the Bread of Life." Which of these has Jesus been to you? And which do you need to ask Him to be in your life? Beloved, He was not just I AM back then; He is still I AM today! He wants to meet your needs and He is your rescuer for every situation!

— DAY 22 —

# THE HELPER

## SEED

*[Jesus said,] "Nevertheless, I tell you the truth: it is to your advantage that I go away, for if I do not go away, the Helper will not come to you. But if I go, I will send him to you."*

—John 16:7 ESV

## CULTIVATE

Read John 14:12–20; 16:7–15; Romans 8:1–17.

## FLOURISH

I've always been fascinated with transformation stories. You know, the ones where the hero or heroine is changed and becomes something they were not before. *Beauty and the Beast*, *Cinderella*, *My Fair Lady*—at the heart of each is a tale of transformation.

Take *My Fair Lady*, for example. In this movie, Eliza Doolittle (played by Audrey Hepburn) is a poor street girl with no money, no education, and no dreams. She's discovered in a wretched state selling flowers in the town square of London. A wager is made, and Professor Henry Higgins takes Eliza under his wing to transform her into a proper lady. He boasts:

> You see this creature with her curbstone English, the English that will keep her in the gutter until the end of her

> days? I say, within six months I could pass her off as a duchess at the Embassy Ball.[1]

My favorite scene is when Eliza departs Professor Higgins's home for the royal ball dressed like a queen. Her makeover is complete. The former dirty street girl is a new woman. But her transformation is not just one of dress and dialect. She sees herself differently, and Eliza gracefully walks out the door as a lady.

Eliza Doolittle's transformation strikes a chord in the human heart—this chord is tuned to the eternal song of redemption. Redemption means to buy something back and to restore it to its original intent. Images of HGTV home makeovers fill my mind as I think of restoration. Like *My Fair Lady*, in these programs, the broken is made beautiful. While these shows are entertaining, the Bible promises the ultimate makeover! Those who trust in Jesus become "new creations" (see 2 Cor. 5:17). We are redeemed from sin, restored to fellowship with the Father, and then transformed by the power of the Holy Spirit.

Randy Alcorn states:

> God is the ultimate salvage artist. He loves to restore things to their original condition—and make them even better.[2]

But how does this spiritual transformation take place? Jesus described the initial stage of this process in the Gospel of John. He began by addressing how we are restored to relationship with God before introducing the Divine Agent of our transformation—the Holy Spirit. Jesus declared:

---

1 G. Cukor, dir., *My Fair Lady*, Warner Bros., 1964.

2 Alcorn, *Heaven*, 89.

*If anyone thirsts, let him come to Me and drink. He who believes in Me, as the Scripture has said, out of his heart will flow rivers of living water.*

—John 7:37 NKJV

Jesus made this announcement while at the annual Jewish Feast of Tabernacles, a time when the Israelites celebrated how the Lord provided for their every need during their forty-year wilderness journey. On the last and "greatest day of the festival" (John 7:37 NIV), the high priest led the people in a procession from the Temple through Jerusalem to the pool of Siloam. The priest filled a pitcher with water, and the procession continued back to the Temple. He then poured the water out onto the altar as an act of worship that acknowledged God alone as the Giver of life.

It was during this ceremony that Jesus revealed He was the Living Water for the thirsty soul. Jesus invites thirsty souls to "come and drink." "To drink" means "to believe." Friends, this invitation is more than mere intellectual knowledge. To drink implies experience, trust, and dependence upon Him. When we come to Jesus and drink of the Living Water, we forsake other fountains, admitting that they will never truly satisfy.

Notice what Jesus said next: "'Whoever believes in me, as the Scripture has said, "Out of his heart will flow rivers of living water."' Now this he said about the Spirit, whom those who believed in him were to receive, for as yet the Spirit had not been given, because Jesus was not yet glorified" (John 7:38–39 ESV).

Jesus used a river to symbolize the Spirit of God filling the human soul. The Holy Spirit is given to all who place their faith in Christ; this is when our spiritual transformation begins. God's Spirit takes up residence in our hearts and begins an internal renovation. The indwelling power of the Spirit fulfills the promise

God made through the prophets to establish a New Covenant. The Old Covenant, given to Israel on Mount Sinai, was written on stone. The New Covenant, given through faith in Jesus, is written on our hearts by the power of the Spirit (see Ezek. 36:26–27).

Christianity is not a self-improvement religion in which one tries hard to do better and to work harder, or strives to be good in their own strength. We can't fix ourselves. We desperately need Jesus to save us, and we require the Holy Spirit to change us. Therefore, Jesus called the Holy Spirit our Helper—because we can't do it ourselves! (See John 16:7–15.)

So, who is the Holy Spirit? He is the third person of the Trinity. The orthodox Christian belief concerning God is that He is one in essence yet three in persons: *Father, Son, and Holy Spirit.* Each person of the Trinity is fully God and plays a unique role in our salvation. It is the primary role of the Holy Spirit to restore us to the image of God.

Recall that after Adam and Eve rebelled in the Garden of Eden, sin fractured the image of God in man. Sin also brought devastating consequences like shame, death, and fear. In addition, the connection between the human spirit and God's Spirit was broken. From that point on, we've been captives to our sinful nature and can't glorify God as we were designed to do. With the gift of the Holy Spirit, not only is the curse of sin broken by Jesus, but we are now reconnected to God and have the internal power of the Spirit that enables us to live for His glory!

Jesus told us that the Holy Spirit is our Helper. As we've surveyed the Bible from garden to garden, one truth is painfully obvious: Humanity needs help! While we were created to be God's image-bearers, we are broken by sin! This is where the Holy Spirit comes in to do what we can't do because the Spirit desires more than anything else to glorify God. Therefore, here are the amazing ways the Holy Spirit helps us when He takes up residence in us:

- He convicts us of sin so we can trust Jesus as our Savior.
- He gives us new power to resist sin and to walk in God's light.
- He enables us to live for God's glory.
- He illuminates the Bible, so we can understand it.
- He produces Christlike character in us and imparts spiritual gifts to us to further the Kingdom of God across the globe.
- He pours God's love into our hearts so we can love others with it.

When we have the Holy Spirit, we have all we need. For this reason, Jesus told the disciples that it was to their benefit that He went away so that the Holy Spirit could be sent to them. As A. W. Tozer writes, "The Spirit-filled life is not a special, deluxe edition of Christianity. It is part and parcel of the total plan of God for His people."[3]

We will look at the outpouring of the Spirit in a few days as we continue our survey of the Bible, but for now, keep in mind that the Holy Spirit is God's agent of transformation. He is the One who works in every believer to restore us as image-bearers of God. Just as Eliza Doolittle was transformed from a dirty street beggar to a beautiful lady, so, too, by the power of the Holy Spirit, we are transformed by God's grace to reflect His glory.

> *In him you also, when you heard the word of truth, the gospel of your salvation, and believed in him, were sealed with the promised Holy Spirit, who is the guarantee of our inheritance until we acquire possession of it, to the praise of his glory.*
>
> —Ephesians 1:13–14 ESV

3 A. W. Tozer, *How to Be Filled with the Holy Spirit* (Chicago: Moody Publishers, 2016), 39.

## HARVEST

Pause to consider Jesus' encouragement: "It is to your advantage that I go away, for if I do not go away, the Helper will not come to you" (John 16:7 ESV). How incredible must the Holy Spirit be if Jesus thought it was better for us to have the indwelling power of the Holy Spirit rather than His physical presence with us? Review the ways the Holy Spirit is our Helper. What specifically do you need to ask for help with today? Take time to turn that honest confession into a prayer.

DAY 23

# THE VINE AND THE BRANCHES

## SEED

*I am the vine; you are the branches. If you remain in me and I in you, you will bear much fruit; apart from me you can do nothing.*

—John 15:5 NIV

## CULTIVATE

Read John 13–15.

## FLOURISH

Torches and twilight marked the path as Jesus' disciples followed Him toward their destination. They trudged along the stone-covered path with heavy hearts due to the weighty conversation that had taken place during that evening's Passover meal. Jesus warned of His looming arrest, betrayals, and how He would die. Then, as Jesus took the bread and wine, He demonstrated the New Covenant that would come through His suffering and death. The bread, His body broken for us; the wine, His blood spilled for us. While the disciples were bewildered, none of these events took Jesus by surprise.

A heavy cloak of sadness covered them as they walked across Jerusalem toward the Garden of Gethsemane. Jesus realized this was His last night with His followers before His arrest, so He paused at a vineyard to share a vital truth with them.

In my opinion, a person's last words are important. Final thoughts, farewells, and instructions are often given in these moments. If the final words are from Jesus Christ, then I think we should pay particular attention. On this fateful night, He sought to encourage and equip those who would carry His Gospel message to the world after His death and resurrection.

Keep in mind that Jesus journeyed with this group for three years. During that time, He taught them many things: Forgive those who hurt you because you, too, have been forgiven. Love others because love fulfills God's law. Live humbly because pride is the root of all sin. And Jesus also taught us to not judge by externals but rather to look at a person's heart. On this night, just hours before His arrest, He shared the number one thing they would need to know going forward.

The Christian life is not merely agreeing with a certain set of theological facts (although what we believe is vitally important to our faith) or attempting to adopt proper behavior; what makes our faith truly remarkable is our union with God. Through Christ we are reconciled and brought back into relational oneness with God the Father. This divine union is made possible only by Jesus, who came from heaven to earth to serve as our access to eternal life (see John 14:6). This is the spiritual reality Jesus illustrated to His disciples by utilizing a common grapevine. Jesus said:

> *I am the true vine, and my Father is the vinedresser. Every branch in me that does not bear fruit he takes away, and every branch that does bear fruit he prunes, that it may bear more fruit. Already you are clean because of the word that I have spoken to you. Abide in me, and I in you. As the branch cannot bear fruit by itself, unless it abides in the*

*vine, neither can you, unless you abide in me. I am the vine; you are the branches. Whoever abides in me and I in him, he it is that bears much fruit, for apart from me you can do nothing.*

—John 15:1–5 ESV

How fitting that He used a garden setting to illustrate this teaching. After all, He describes an Edenic existence, where we walk with God, live in His Presence, and draw life from Him. In this illustration, the Father is the Gardener, or as some translations say, "the vinedresser." This means God the Father is tending and watching over the Vine and His branches to ensure they thrive, produce fruit, and are protected from the elements.

In this divine connection, Jesus is the Vine, and His followers are the branches. Just as a branch depends on the vine for life, so do we rely on Him. Just as a grapevine is rooted in the earth's soil and sends nutrients to the branches, producing grapes, Jesus is rooted in the soil of heaven and sends His life to us, the branches. When we remain connected to Him, His Holy Spirit flows in us and through us, and the outcome is a bounty of spiritual fruit.

*But the fruit of the Spirit is love, joy, peace, patience, kindness, goodness, faithfulness, gentleness, self-control; against such things there is no law.*

—Galatians 5:22–23 ESV

The key to this relationship is dependence. For people who take pride in independence, this one can be difficult, but the secret to the abundant Christian life is found in declaring our absolute dependence on Jesus. As verse 4 of John 15 says, "Abide in me, and I in you. As the branch cannot bear fruit by itself, unless it abides in the vine, neither can you, unless you abide in me" (ESV). Unless we rely on Jesus for everything, we will not bear fruit. Period. I can't produce love, joy, peace, patience, kindness, goodness, faithfulness, gentleness, and self-control on my own. I must be connected to my life Source. I need Jesus.

This leads us to the million-dollar question: How do we stay connected to Christ if He is not physically present with us? As we learned yesterday, those who believe in Jesus receive the Holy Spirit to live in us and empower us. God's Spirit is the supernatural life that flows from Jesus to us and enables us to live for God's glory. When we stay connected to Him through prayer—relying on the Spirit's power when tempted and seeking His leading in decisions and spending time *daily* in God's Word, the Bible—then our lives bear fruit.

> *[Jesus said,] "If you abide in me, and my words abide in you, ask whatever you wish, and it will be done for you. By this my Father is glorified, that you bear much fruit and so prove to be my disciples."*
>
> —John 15:7–8 ESV

When we spend consistent time in the Word of God, we are connected to Christ. His words fill us, guide us, and allow the Holy Spirit to produce fruit in us. The Christian life is not one of imitation, where we strive to be like Jesus. Rather, the Christian life is one of participation, where we are joined to the Lord and our mind, will, and emotions become one with His.

Jesus shared this teaching with a clear purpose: "These things I have spoken to you, that my joy may be in you, and that your joy may be full" (John 15:11 ESV). Joy is the overflow of life with God. In a world where people chase happiness with the next purchase, the next relationship, or the next substance…true and lasting joy is available when we draw life from the Source.

Through a relationship with Jesus, what was lost in the Garden of Eden is restored. Connected to Christ, we experience the shalom of God's Presence. As we abide in this divine relationship, we are nourished with life that flows from the Holy Spirit and experience the Father's love that waters the soil of our hearts. As we abide in Christ, we flourish like a fruitful branch that is connected to the Vine.

Although the disciples couldn't comprehend all that was about to happen in the coming hours and days before Jesus' death and resurrection, He wanted them to know that in the end, He would fulfill the mission that He came to accomplish. He would redeem humanity from the clutches of sin and death and restore us to the garden, to our true home—with God.

> *By this my Father is glorified, that you bear much fruit and so prove to be my disciples.*
>
> —John 15:8 ESV

## HARVEST

Perhaps you are finding yourself disconnected from the Vine (Jesus). Be honest with God and yourself: In what ways have you lived independently or self-sufficiently? What steps can you take to be a branch that is connected to the Vine? What practical changes can you make to "abide" in Jesus throughout the day?

— DAY 24 —

# THE LAMB OF GOD

## — SEED

*The next day he saw Jesus coming toward him, and said, "Behold, the Lamb of God, who takes away the sin of the world!"*

—John 1:29 ESV

## — CULTIVATE

Read John 18–19.

## — FLOURISH

The moment humanity had longed for since the Garden of Eden had finally arrived. The Redeemer, the promised "Seed of the woman," whom God said would crush the Serpent, stood ready to face the Enemy. The week leading up to this monumental moment was tumultuous. It began with Jesus' triumphal entry as the Messiah into Jerusalem, as worshippers thronged the ancient pathway shouting:

> *Hosanna! Blessed is he who comes in the name of the Lord,*
> *even the King of Israel!*
>
> —John 12:13 ESV

However, their praises quickly fell to silence as Jesus faced a week of testing by the religious authorities. Although they continuously accused Him, "he committed no sin, neither was deceit found in his mouth" (1 Pet. 2:22 ESV). Jesus was sinless, but that fact didn't stop those who wanted to get rid of Him. They would not be stopped in their obsession to destroy Jesus.

The events we study today center upon the holiest day of the Jewish calendar—the Feast of Passover. This feast celebrated how God redeemed Israel from slavery in Egypt with the blood of the lamb. Recall how Moses instructed the people to sacrifice a spotless lamb and apply its blood to their homes so the angel of death would pass over them. Jesus understood He was the fulfillment of everything the Passover lamb symbolized. His blood was the ultimate covering that brought life instead of death, and His sacrificial death would bring deliverance from slavery to sin.

Jesus was fully aware of His mission. He understood He must die as the Passover Lamb. Therefore, as the hours grew closer to the feast, Jesus prepared the disciples for the suffering He would endure. It's important to remember that even though Jesus understood, that didn't make the physical, emotional, and spiritual agony easy. After all, He was also fully human.

The Gospel of John tells us that Jesus was with His disciples in the Garden of Gethsemane on the eve of Passover. Surrounded by ancient olive trees, He prayed and sought strength from His Heavenly Father. How perfectly fitting that the place where Jesus surrendered His will to serve as our Savior occurred in a garden. The story has come full circle. Christ's entrance into this garden reminds us of Eden.

In the Garden of Eden, Adam experienced paradise, but in Gethsemane, Jesus experienced agony. In Eden, Adam walked with God, enjoyed the bounty, and knew nothing of sorrow or pain. In Gethsemane, Jesus sweat drops of blood, cried out to God, and agonized over the torture He knew would soon occur.

In Eden, Adam hid, but in Gethsemane, Jesus boldly stepped forward and walked toward His destiny.

The quiet, dark Jerusalem night was interrupted by a mob marching into Gethsemane. Hundreds of Roman soldiers and Jewish religious authorities came to capture one man. Jesus knew it was His hour, and instead of running, He stepped forward to meet them. Sadly, Judas, one of His disciples, led the mob to find Jesus. With swords drawn, the soldiers pressed into the garden. Jesus stepped forward and said: "'Whom do you seek?' They answered him, 'Jesus of Nazareth'" (John 18:5 ESV).

What happened next is my all-time favorite scene in the entire Bible. I love it because Jesus merely said, "I am he" (John 18:5 ESV), and when He did, the Roman soldiers and pompous religious elite fell flat on their faces! What caused them to face-plant? The unveiling of His glory! God Almighty, the Creator of heaven and earth, spoke His name! When Jesus said, "I am," He uttered the sacred, holy name of God—Yahweh! The name spoken to Moses at the burning bush came from Jesus; when it did, those present couldn't stand in the face of such glory!

This scene reveals who Jesus is. He is the Lamb of God who willingly laid down His life as our Savior. They did not take Him against His will. No, He offered Himself as the Passover Lamb. This moment revealed His glorious power and grace. Although He could have uttered a word and annihilated His captors, He instead allowed them to arrest Him so He could go to a cross for them.

Jesus faced beatings, false accusations, and corrupt trials in the wee hours of the morning before sunrise. In the end, He was sentenced to death by crucifixion. Pontius Pilate, the Roman governor, turned the Son of God over to men who brutally tortured Him. Then they forced Him to carry His cross to a hill outside of the city where He would be crucified. Nails were driven into the hands that healed lepers, and the feet that walked on water were hammered to a tree. They nailed Jesus to His cross, where he was surrounded by thieves and mocked by onlookers (see John 19:18). As Jesus bled, struggled to breathe, and took on the punishment for humanity's sin, the sky turned black. Heaven mourned.

This form of capital punishment was reserved for the lowest kind of criminals. Today we see the cross as a symbol of glory and victory, but in Roman times, the cross stood for ultimate rejection, shame, and suffering. Friend, that's exactly what Jesus bore for us. He took our sin punishment, our shame, so that we could take on His righteousness, forgiveness, and status as God's beloved child. We call this the great exchange.

I've often heard it said, "Something is worth what someone is willing to pay for it." Whether it is a car, a house, or a painting… the value of that item is derived based upon what someone is willing to pay for it. As we ponder Jesus on the cross, we must absorb the reality of what occurred on that fateful day. Your worth and mine were established. Jesus stepped out of heaven and entered our broken human story knowing the suffering that awaited Him on that Roman cross. And why did He endure such a horrific death? Because He was willing to pay the highest price to redeem you. Friend, let this truth soak in…God said that you were worth dying for.

John, the beloved disciple of Jesus who penned an eyewitness account, watched in horror as the final moments of Jesus' life slipped away. He shared with us Jesus' final words on the cross: Jesus said, "'It is finished,' and he bowed his head and gave up his spirit" (John 19:30 ESV).

*It is finished.* These words are the climax of human history. Since the fatal fall of man into sin in the Garden of Eden, the world has desperately longed for redemption. With Jesus' death on the cross, the prophetic promise concerning the "Seed of the woman" was realized. The Serpent indeed did "strike his heel," with Roman nails driving through Jesus' flesh. But this mortal wound would bring about his ultimate defeat as our Redeemer crushed his head! Friends, we close today with heavy hearts as we contemplate the depths of God's love for us in giving His Son to die for us. But we must remember, Sunday's coming!

> *Yet it was our weaknesses he carried;*
> *it was our sorrows that weighed him down.*
> *And we thought his troubles were a punishment from God,*
> *a punishment for his own sins!*
> *But he was pierced for our rebellion,*
> *crushed for our sins.*
> *He was beaten so we could be whole.*
> *He was whipped so we could be healed.*
> *All of us, like sheep, have strayed away.*
> *We have left God's paths to follow our own.*
> *Yet the* LORD *laid on him*
> *the sins of us all.*
>
> —Isaiah 53:4–6 NLT

## HARVEST

It is heart-wrenching to consider the suffering Jesus endured on the cross. It's impossible for us to grasp the agony and pain He willingly accepted as He took on the sins of the world. My sins. Your sins. It's unimaginable. But we don't read and remember this scene to bring guilt upon ourselves. Quite the opposite! Jesus' sacrifice demonstrates God's tremendous love for us and the depths to which He went to rescue us and offer our salvation. Take some time to thank God for the sacrifice Jesus made on your behalf and what that means for your life. Oh, how He loves you.

DAY 25

# THE RESURRECTED KING

## SEED

*Why do you seek the living among the dead? He is not here, but has risen. Remember how he told you, while he was still in Galilee, that the Son of Man must be delivered into the hands of sinful men and be crucified and on the third day rise.*

—Luke 24:5–7 ESV

## CULTIVATE

Read John 20; Romans 6:5–6.

## FLOURISH

It was early on Sunday when Mary Magdalene slipped into the cold Jerusalem morning. Her destination was the garden tomb where Jesus was buried. Mary was a follower of Christ and stood watch near the cross with His mother as Jesus died. Three days later, she was the first to the tomb. The other disciples were hiding in fear, but not Mary. Only one thing was on her mind—Jesus. As she hurried toward the tomb, she likely recalled the first day she saw Him.

Jesus entered her village and transformed her life. Everyone had heard about Him, but now she would see the One whom many believed was the Messiah, who would make all things new. That's exactly what Jesus did for Mary.

Mary Magdalene had been possessed by seven demons (see Luke 8:2). A poster child for Satan's schemes, she was afflicted by an evil that left her hopeless for change. We aren't told how, but we know Mary encountered Jesus and was delivered. From that moment on, she devoted her life to following Him.

As she hurried toward the garden she likely thought, *He cast seven demons out of me, yet didn't save His own life? I'm living proof that He had the power—why did He submit to such a death? It doesn't seem right.* Some see Jesus' death as a tragedy—questioning why a man who did so much for others died so brutally. But all those questions miss the point. Jesus came to die. That was His mission.

The most important truth in the world is this—death didn't win! Jesus rose from the grave, the firstfruits of a New Creation for the glory of God! But to fully appreciate what Mary Magdalene experienced that first Easter, we must begin with the fact that Jesus truly died.

On that fateful Friday, when Jesus said, "It is finished," and took His last breath, hell rejoiced because Satan thought he'd won. The Serpent wrongly believed he had rid the world of the Son of God. While the sun set over Jerusalem, Jesus' lifeless body was wrapped in burial spices and linen. Mary Magdalene and His mother watched as two righteous men carried Jesus' body to a nearby garden, where they placed Him in a tomb. Then, the Roman governor ordered a massive stone to seal the entrance and posted guards to watch over it.

As Ken Gire describes it,

It was in a garden, ages ago that paradise was lost,
and it is in a garden now that it would be regained.[1]

It is to that garden tomb that Mary Magdalene hurried that Sunday morning. Friends, we come again to a garden, a strange place for a tomb unless God Himself is the Author of this story. After all, it was in the Garden of Eden that the curse of death first fell on humanity, and at the garden tomb, the curse was broken!

To grasp the fullness of what the Bible reveals, consider what transpires in nature in a garden. First, a seed is planted into the soil of the earth. Next, the seed dies, and the outer shell breaks open—new life sprouts up, begins to grow, and ascends toward the light above the surface, until it finally breaks free.

This is the redemption story we've been following since sin entered the world in the Garden of Eden. Jesus is the promised "Seed of the woman" (see Gen. 3:15). His dead body was taken from the cross and placed inside a tomb, the soil of the earth. Three days later, by the miraculous power of the Holy Spirit, new life sprang up and He rose from the grave. The mystery of Christ's death and resurrection is literally woven into the very fabric of nature, and it occurred just as Jesus prophesied:

*I tell you the truth, unless a kernel of wheat is planted in the soil and dies, it remains alone. But its death will produce many new kernels—a plentiful harvest of new lives.*

—John 12:24 NLT

This brings us back to Sunday morning when Mary Magdalene found the stone rolled away. Baffled, she ran back to tell the others

---

1 Ken Gire, *Moments with the Savior* (Grand Rapids, MI: Zondervan, 1998), 379.

(see John 20:2). Hearing her wild report, John and Peter raced to the garden and found the scene just as Mary had described. What they saw next, what they beheld in that empty tomb, absolutely wrecked them—in the best way!

> *Then Simon Peter arrived and went inside. He also noticed the linen wrappings lying there, while the cloth that had covered Jesus' head was folded up and lying apart from the other wrappings. Then the disciple who had reached the tomb first also went in, and he saw and believed.*
>
> —John 20:6–8 NLT

What did John see? What was so convincing that he would never recant his testimony or back down from proclaiming the resurrection?

Warren Wiersbe tells us:

> John saw the burial wrappings lying in the shape of the body, but the body was gone! The graveclothes lay like an empty cocoon. The napkin (for the face) was carefully folded, lying by itself. It was not the scene of a grave robbery, for no robbers could have gotten the body out of the graveclothes without tearing the cloth and disarranging things. Jesus had returned to life in power and glory and had passed through the graveclothes and the tomb itself![2]

Although many falsely accused the disciples of fabricating this story, their testimonies show that, in fact, they were surprised

---

2 Warren W. Wiersbe, *Wiersbe's Expository Outlines on the New Testament* (Wheaton, IL: Victor Books, 1992), 266.

that Jesus was not in the tomb. When John saw the graveclothes looking like an empty cocoon from which Jesus had emerged, it was then that he believed, without a doubt, that Jesus had risen from the dead. While both had been devoted disciples before, from that point on, they would be unwavering believers that Jesus Christ is the Lord God Almighty, the resurrected King.

John's faith was validated later that night when "the disciples were meeting behind locked doors because they were afraid of the Jewish leaders. Suddenly, Jesus was standing there among them! 'Peace be with you,' he said. As he spoke, he showed them the wounds in his hands and his side. They were filled with joy when they saw the Lord!" (John 20:19–20 NLT). John not only saw the empty graveclothes, but he also beheld the resurrected King.

The resurrection of Jesus is a proven historical fact. Billy Graham wrote, "There is more evidence that Jesus rose from the dead than there is that Julius Caesar ever lived or that Alexander the Great died at the age of thirty-three."[3] More than five hundred eyewitnesses beheld the resurrected Christ, but most important, those witnesses demonstrated a new power as a result of their relationship with Him. John, the beloved disciple, was one of those witnesses. John touched Jesus. He ate meals with Him, heard Him teach about the Kingdom, and watched in wonder as Jesus ascended on the cloud of glory to heaven. John shared his eyewitness testimony of beholding the risen King for one reason—that we would believe and experience the resurrected life in Christ!

Over the last ten days as we've beheld Emmanuel, we've come to recognize Jesus is the "Seed of the woman" who was first promised in the Garden of Eden. He faithfully crushed the head of the Serpent with His sacrificial death and won victory with His

---

3 "Peace with God—Why Jesus Came," Billy Graham Library, March 25, 2021, https://billygrahamlibrary.org/blog-peace-with-god-why-jesus-came/.

glorious resurrection. We've also witnessed the amazing fulfillment of God's word to Abraham that promised the world would be blessed through one of his descendants. Indeed, through Jesus Christ, who gives eternal life to those who place their faith in Him, the world is truly blessed.

Today we beheld Jesus, the resurrected King, who fulfilled God's covenant with King David that one of his descendants would rule over the Kingdom of God forever (see 1 Chron. 17:11–14). After Jesus rose from the dead, He ascended to His throne in heaven where He now reigns on high. Friends, marvel at the Word of God! From Eden through the long arduous years of exile, all these messianic prophecies find their fulfillment in Emmanuel.

God's redemption story doesn't end here. Oh, no! Jesus' victory over sin and death launched a new day, birthed a new people, and offers new life for the children of God. Jesus was the firstfruits of the New Creation and now the collected body of believers across the globe is called the Church. We are the people of God who hope in the promises of God. As we turn the page to discover the rest of the story, we will look at some essential truths that mark the Church and feast on glorious promises concerning our eternity.

> *But Christ has indeed been raised from the dead, the firstfruits of those who have fallen asleep. For since death came through a man, the resurrection of the dead comes also through a man. For as in Adam all die, so in Christ all will be made alive. But each in turn: Christ, the firstfruits; then, when he comes, those who belong to him.*
>
> —1 Corinthians 15:20–23 NIV

## HARVEST

The evidence for the resurrection is overwhelming. The disciples were transformed because of beholding Jesus, the risen King of Kings and Lord of Lords. Jesus is called the "firstfruits" because He is the first of the New Creation. The Bible makes clear that those who place their faith in Jesus will also experience the resurrection. How does this promise transform your outlook on life, death, and eternity?

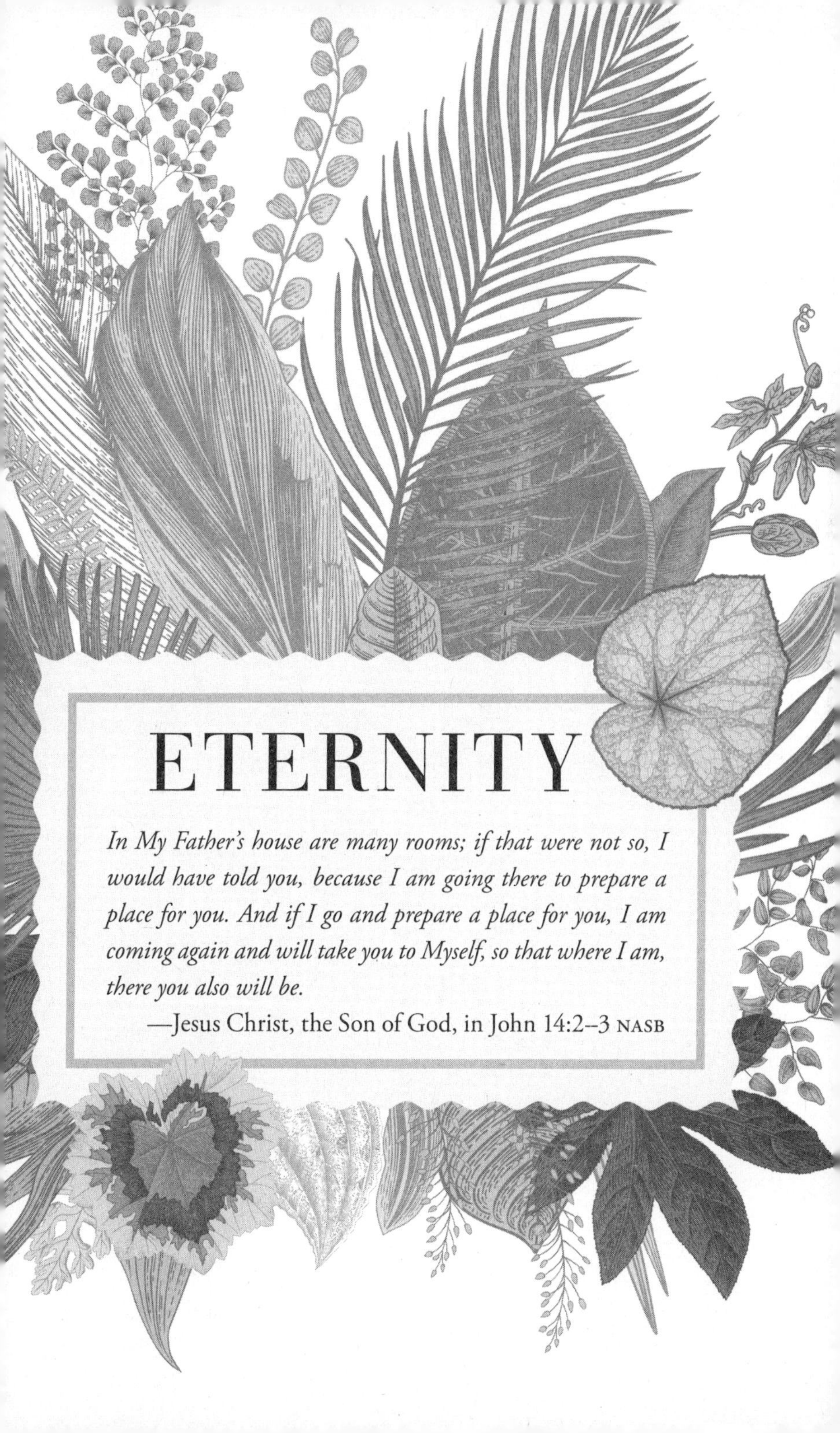

# ETERNITY

*In My Father's house are many rooms; if that were not so, I would have told you, because I am going there to prepare a place for you. And if I go and prepare a place for you, I am coming again and will take you to Myself, so that where I am, there you also will be.*

—Jesus Christ, the Son of God, in John 14:2–3 NASB

DAY 26

# THE FATHER'S LOVE

## SEED

*See what kind of love the Father has given to us, that we should be called children of God; and so we are. The reason why the world does not know us is that it did not know him.*

—1 John 3:1 ESV

## CULTIVATE

Read Matthew 6:9–13; 18:12–14; James 1:17.

## FLOURISH

I love a good redemption story. Especially one that illustrates the glorious redemption narrative revealed in Scripture. One of my all-time favorites is the movie *Taken*. While I'm not typically a fan of action movies (I'm more of a Jane Austen kind of girl), this is my go-to movie when teaching about the lavish love that God the Father has for us. For *Taken* illustrates the lengths to which God the Father went to rescue and restore us as His own.

*Taken* is about a teenage girl whose dad is a retired government operative who is extremely skilled in intelligence operations. His background and training cause him to be highly protective when his daughter, who is only seventeen, seeks his permission to spend the summer in Paris with a friend.

Aware of the dangers they could encounter, her protective dad says no. But he later changes his mind and allows the trip if she promises to follow his rules and abide by his terms. Unfortunately, upon their arrival in Paris, the girls ignore his warnings and are kidnapped by a criminal sex-trafficking ring. A father's worst nightmare has occurred. His daughter is taken by perverted men with evil intentions. He must act—and quickly. *Taken* reveals a man on a mission to save his daughter.

I sat breathless on the edge of my seat watching this film. My pulse quickened as the father vowed his intention to rescue her from the wicked men. My stomach sickened as I realized she was sold into sex trafficking. I cheered out loud as her father systematically tracked down the villains and kicked down doors to reach his daughter locked inside. Then, tears streamed down my face at the end when her captor realized, "It's the girl's father, and he wants her back."

Friends, please don't miss that line! All the action, adventure, and heroics are about one thing—a father rescuing his beloved child. Most importantly, this is the message of the whole Bible! The Bible is the story of God's rescue mission.

All that Jesus accomplished on the cross and validated through His resurrection must be seen through the eyes of God the Father, who loved us so lavishly that He sent His beloved Son as our Redeemer.

> *For God so loved the world, that he gave his only Son, that whoever believes in him should not perish but have eternal life.*
>
> —John 3:16 ESV

Jesus' death was the ransom payment that released us from captivity, setting us free from Satan, sin, and death. But that's not all; the Word of God tells us that we aren't just forgiven people—we are now children of God, adopted into His family. All that was lost in Eden is restored through Jesus. This was the divine plan of God the Father from the very beginning (see Eph. 1:3–6).

This glorious truth brings us back to where we left off yesterday. Mary Magdalene was the first and the last at the tomb of Jesus Christ. Peter and John left in astonishment after seeing the empty graveclothes. However, Mary lingered in the garden. Overcome with grief, she stepped into the tomb, where she was greeted by two angels who asked, "Woman, why are you weeping?" (John 20:13 ESV).

Mary explained that she was searching for Jesus' body and then turned to find a man standing before her. Her eyes were flooded with tears, and she didn't recognize that it was the risen Lord standing before her. Assuming He was the gardener, she pleaded with Him to show her where Jesus' body was taken.

Then Jesus spoke her name, "Mary." At the sound of His voice, she knew it was the Lord and exclaimed, "Teacher!" Jesus said to her, "Do not cling to me, for I have not yet ascended to the Father; but go to my brothers and say to them, 'I am ascending to my Father and your Father, to my God and your God'" (John 20:17 ESV).

Mary Magdalene was the first eyewitness of His resurrection and proclaimer of His victory. In Jesus' directions to Mary, we find the heart of the redemption story. Jesus called God His Father and *her* Father.

This is the radical result of Christ's resurrection—a woman who was once captive to seven demons is now a child of God! Formerly, we were separated from God because of sin, but those who trust in Jesus as their Savior are adopted into the family of God.

> *To all who did receive him, who believed in his name, he gave the right to become children of God, who were born, not of blood nor of the will of the flesh nor of the will of man, but of God.*
>
> —John 1:12–13 ESV

This is the Gospel, and it changes everything. Not only does it change our status from sinner to saint, but it also gives us a new identity—beloved child of God. All throughout the New Testament, we are taught to approach God with confidence, without fear, because we are welcomed into His Presence. We are encouraged to bring our every need to our Heavenly Father who loves us. We are reminded that our God gives good gifts to His children. Relating to God as Father is a game changer!

Theologian J. I. Packer described the enormity of this new reality the best:

> You sum up the whole of New Testament religion if you describe it as the knowledge of God as one's holy Father. If you want to judge how well a person understands Christianity, find out how much he makes of the thought of being God's child, and having God as his Father. If this is not the thought that prompts and controls his worship and prayers and his whole outlook on life, it means that he does not understand Christianity very well at all.
>
> For everything that Christ taught, everything that makes the New Testament new, and better than the Old, everything that is distinctively Christian as opposed to

> merely Jewish, is summed up in the knowledge of the Fatherhood of God. "Father" is the Christian name for God. Our understanding of Christianity cannot be better than our grasp of adoption.[1]

Jesus came and died and rose again for one purpose: to reconcile us to the Father. After we believe, the Holy Spirit indwells us, and we now relate to God as His beloved child. No longer are we striving to earn a place through keeping rules or following religion. No—in Christ, we are forever part of God's family. Through the indwelling Spirit we no longer know God from a distance, but as our *Abba*, which is the Hebrew word for "Daddy."

Friend, I don't know what your relationship was like with your earthly father. He may have been absent or indifferent, but your Heavenly Father is One who moved heaven and earth to redeem you! The Bible says that before the foundation of the world, God saw you, He chose you, and He sent His beloved Son to rescue you! Friend, you are the apple of His eye!

> *For all who are led by the Spirit of God are sons of God. For you did not receive the spirit of slavery to fall back into fear, but you have received the Spirit of adoption as sons, by whom we cry, "Abba! Father!" The Spirit himself bears witness with our spirit that we are children of God.*
>
> —Romans 8:14–16 ESV

1 J. I. Packer, *Knowing God* (United Kingdom: InterVarsity Press, 2021), 202.

## HARVEST

Do you easily relate to God as your Heavenly Father? This is the privilege we can enjoy through Jesus Christ. Bear this truth in mind: The Father delights in you, He chose you, and He sent His Son to redeem you. The Father doesn't view you with apathy, indifference, or disappointment. No, He calls you His beloved child! Take a minute to sit before God and call Him Abba Father. Bring any concerns or cares on your heart to Him.

### DAY 27

# THE CHURCH IS BORN

## SEED

*When the day of Pentecost arrived, they were all together in one place. And suddenly there came from heaven a sound like a mighty rushing wind, and it filled the entire house where they were sitting.*

—Acts 2:1–2 ESV

## CULTIVATE

Read Acts 1–2.

## FLOURISH

I live in Texas, and we experienced a long drought this summer. The grass was brown and thirsty, and our little family garden was barely making it. Therefore, we were more than a little excited recently when the weatherman reported a storm on the horizon. As the clouds rolled in, we huddled up on the couch to watch the much-needed rain fall and soak the dry land. With the storm came a good bit of lightning and thunder. In the distance, we watched lightning bolts flash across the Texas sky and then we waited, and counted 1, 2, 3, 4 for the thunder to boom.

The time lapse between a lightning strike and a thunder crash perfectly illustrates what happened between Jesus' resurrection and the outpouring of the Holy Spirit on the day of Pentecost. While these two cosmic events were divinely connected, there was an interval between them. Jesus' resurrection was the lightning bolt that pierced the eternal sky and brought His victory over sin and death. His glorious resurrection was then followed by a period of waiting, fifty days to be exact, until the sound of thunder, as the promised Holy Spirit was given to the disciples.

In between these two world-changing events, Jesus ascended into heaven. The ascension occurred forty days after His resurrection when Jesus and His disciples gathered on the Mount of Olives in Jerusalem. More than five hundred people were eyewitnesses of the risen Christ. As the disciples gathered, many asked Him if it was the time for Him to usher in the Kingdom.

It should be noted that the early disciples were expecting an earthly Kingdom, like that of King David. Instead, Jesus established a spiritual Kingdom, where men and women across the globe are rescued from Satan's domain of darkness and by faith become citizens of the Kingdom of God (see Col. 1:13). Jesus' disciples are sent into the world as His ambassadors on earth (see Matt. 28:18–20). But Jesus said that this Great Commission would be accomplished only by the Holy Spirit's power. Which is why He said:

> *You will receive power when the Holy Spirit has come upon you, and you will be my witnesses in Jerusalem and in all Judea and Samaria, and to the end of the earth.*
>
> —Acts 1:8 ESV

Jesus told the disciples to wait in Jerusalem until the outpouring of the Spirit. Then, Jesus blessed them and ascended before their eyes into heaven on a cloud (see Luke 24:50–51; Acts 1:9–11).

As the disciples watched in wonder, they were told by angels that this "same Jesus" would return in the very same way—on a cloud of glory. The astonished men and women returned to Jerusalem and waited for the promised Holy Spirit, who would empower them to be His witnesses to the ends of the earth. Our SEED passage describes the dramatic moment when God's Spirit was poured out upon the early Church:

> *When the day of Pentecost arrived, they were all together in one place. And suddenly there came from heaven a sound like a mighty rushing wind, and it filled the entire house where they were sitting. And divided tongues as of fire appeared to them and rested on each one of them. And they were all filled with the Holy Spirit and began to speak in other tongues as the Spirit gave them utterance.*
>
> —Acts 2:1–4 ESV

Recall in John 7:37–39 that Jesus promised those who believed in Him would receive the Holy Spirit. On Pentecost, that promise was fulfilled. The dynamic power of the resurrected Christ now fills and flows through every believer. The promise of the New Covenant that God's Spirit would indwell us, enabling us to live for God's glory, is now realized. The outpouring of the Holy Spirit marked the birth of the Church.

When many think of the Church, images of stained-glass windows and towering steeples might fill their minds. But the Church is not a building. The Church comprises the people of God from every nation, language, and culture. We are the Body of Christ, filled with the Holy Spirit, who serve as Jesus' Presence on earth (see Eph. 2:21–22). We are entrusted with the message the world is desperate to hear: God came to rescue us from sin and restore us to His Presence.

The book of Acts details how God used the early Church to launch what is now known as Christianity. During their first gathering, three thousand people came to faith in Jesus Christ. And at their second one, over five thousand were added to their number. Biblical historians tell us that six months after Pentecost, there were approximately one hundred thousand Christians in the city of Jerusalem. And here's the astonishing fact: Every single believer today traces our faith back to this gathering that began with a handful of devoted disciples in Acts 2.

> *And they devoted themselves to the apostles' teaching and the fellowship, to the breaking of bread and the prayers. And awe came upon every soul, and many wonders and signs were being done through the apostles. And all who believed were together and had all things in common. And they were selling their possessions and belongings and distributing the proceeds to all, as any had need. And day by day, attending the temple together and breaking bread in their homes, they received their food with glad and generous hearts, praising God and having favor with all the people. And the Lord added to their number day by day those who were being saved.*
>
> —Acts 2:42–47 ESV

Those earliest believers carried the Gospel to the world. Acts describes how the Kingdom of God broke through religious, racial, gender, and national barriers, taking God's grace far and wide.

How did these ordinary men and women accomplish this incredible mission? Surveying the New Testament and studying Church history, I see the undeniable power of the Holy Spirit and faithful obedience to Jesus Christ, who gave His disciples this charge:

*You are the light of the world. A city set on a hill cannot be hidden. Nor do people light a lamp and put it under a basket, but on a stand, and it gives light to all in the house. In the same way, let your light shine before others, so that they may see your good works and give glory to your Father who is in heaven.*

—Matthew 5:14–16 ESV

As the first followers of Christ sought to live for God's glory and practice His teachings, the light of Christ radiated through the Church! They carried the hope of the Gospel to the farthest reaches of the Roman Empire and beyond. They went out healing the sick, casting out demons, adopting orphans, standing against evil, clothing the poor, and feeding the hungry. Through their public witness, they were light in the darkness.

This brings us full circle to God's purpose of the Temple in the Old Testament. Just as the radiant light of God's Shekinah glory filled the Temple in Jerusalem, so God's glorious Holy Spirit fills the Church. As the apostle Paul encouraged the church in Corinth: "Do you not know that you are God's temple and that God's Spirit dwells in you?" (1 Cor. 3:16 ESV).

This brings us to the Church's purpose in this world. Recall that the intricate design of the Old Testament Temple served as a signpost pointing the way back to the Garden of Eden, where Adam and Eve walked with God and enjoyed relationship with Him. The Temple's purpose was to point the way back into this fellowship. Designed with garden imagery and centered on sacrifices that reconciled a holy God and sinful people, the Temple revealed redemption and restoration.

The Church stands today as the Temple of God because we are reconciled with God by the atoning sacrifice of Jesus Christ, and

His Spirit dwells in the Holy of Holies of each heart. As the new dwelling place of God's Spirit, we are now the signpost, showing the world how to be reconciled to God.

As we see the glorious plan of redemption unfold from garden to garden, it is breathtaking to behold God's promise to restore us to His Presence. The Church, made up of every denomination, every race, language, and people group, is now the new dwelling place of God by His Spirit.

Friend, we are no longer exiles, but our eternal garden paradise still awaits us. We are not home yet. But because of Jesus, we can enjoy friendship with the Lord on this earth and fulfill the purpose for which He created us…to reflect His glory to the world. We, the Church, are carriers of glory and living signposts pointing the way back to the garden.

> *So then you are no longer strangers and aliens, but you are fellow citizens with the saints and members of the household of God, built on the foundation of the apostles and prophets, Christ Jesus himself being the cornerstone, in whom the whole structure, being joined together, grows into a holy temple in the Lord. In him you also are being built together into a dwelling place for God by the Spirit.*
>
> —Ephesians 2:19–22 ESV

## HARVEST

Friends, we each play an important part in God's story that is unfolding on earth today! Remember, you are a "holy temple" and a "dwelling place for God." Considering this truth, what is the difference between *going* to church versus *being* the Church? How does this call impact your daily life?

DAY 28

# THE JOURNEY HOME

## SEED

*My sheep hear my voice, and I know them, and they follow me. I give them eternal life, and they will never perish, and no one will snatch them out of my hand.*

—John 10:27–28 ESV

## CULTIVATE

Read John 10:1–28; Psalm 23.

## FLOURISH

"Follow Me!" Those two life-altering words are an invitation from Jesus Christ to leave the familiar shores of this world and take a step of faith to follow Him. For those of us who heed the call, we are never the same. I should know, for I once stood at a crossroads and looked back at the wasted years of a life without Jesus and sensed a deep longing for Eden that beckoned me to surrender to the One who promised to lead me home.

While I grew up in a religious culture, it wasn't until my mid-twenties when I first heard this call for myself. Until that point, I could have told you a few Bible stories and maybe even quoted a verse or two, but what I didn't know was the Lord. While I had often heard information about Jesus, I didn't really *know* Him.

Friend, that's not the case today.

After two decades of walking with Jesus, I've tasted of His goodness and live because of His grace. I've experienced His mercy and the nearness of His Presence. No longer is Jesus simply my Savior; He is my Strength, my Comforter, and my Living Hope. Over the years, I've experienced Jesus as the Friend of sinners, my Great Physician, and the Anchor of my soul. I can tell you one thing for sure—in my book, Jesus has no rival! As one of my all-time favorite worship songs declares:

*All my life You have been faithful*
*And all my life You have been so, so good.*[1]

Experiencing the unrivaled goodness of God begins with following Him. Thirteen times in the Gospels we hear Jesus summon someone to leave behind their old life and take the step of faith to follow Him. Let's be clear—Jesus doesn't coerce or force anyone. It's a personal decision: Each person decides to follow Jesus, the King of Glory, or to continue living for the kingdom of self.

How do people react to this divine invitation? Oh, the responses are varied! But when Jesus called three fishermen—Peter, James, and John—the Bible says, "Immediately they left their nets and followed him" (Matt. 4:20 ESV). After heeding the call, these men walked with Jesus for three years. They weren't alone; the Gospels tell us that women were among those who abandoned all to follow Christ. These men and women beheld

---

1 "Goodness of God," by Jason Ingram, Ed Cash, Brian Mark Johnson, Jenn Louise Johnson, and Ben David Fielding, © So Essential Tunes, Capitol Cmg Paragon, Bethel Music Publishing, Shout! Music Publishing Australia.

His glory, witnessed His miraculous works, heard His Kingdom teachings, and they were transformed in His Presence.

Following Christ is the essence of the Christian life. It is not about knowing Bible stories or learning religious rituals; the Christian life can be boiled down to walking with Jesus. *With* Him. Let that word settle into your soul. Being with God is the goal. After all, isn't that the life we've ached for since our exile from Eden? For Peter, James, and John, leaving "their nets" symbolized forsaking their old lives, for they were fishermen by trade. But when they heard the call, they left their old lives to go wherever Jesus led them. The same proves true today: Following Christ means detaching from our old lives and attaching ourselves to Christ, who is Life itself.

> *[Jesus said,] "If anyone would come after me, let him deny himself and take up his cross and follow me. For whoever would save his life will lose it, but whoever loses his life for my sake will find it."*
>
> —Matthew 16:24–25 ESV

This call to forsake the old and follow Jesus was not just for the twelve disciples who walked with Him two centuries ago. The heart cry of one who rejects the world to follow Christ is this: Jesus is better! We choose Him over the world. As His disciples, we are on a lifelong journey of becoming like Him as we abide in our relationship with Him (see John 15:1–5).

Friend, this is not rote religion, but the great adventure of living in the Kingdom of God. I could never in a million years have scripted the life the Lord planned for me. I had no clue when I heard "Follow Me" what would transpire as He led me out of the brokenness of my sin, through challenging wilderness seasons, up to brilliant mountaintops, and through seasons when I had to trust His heart when I could not see His face.

As we trace the biblical story from garden to garden, we find a call to return to what was lost at the heart of this redemption story. In Eden, Adam and Eve walked with God. Unfortunately, that intimate friendship was lost when sin entered the world. Therefore, when Jesus invites us to follow Him, He beckons us to return to an Edenic state, where we commune with God and enjoy life in His Presence.

A brief survey of Scripture reveals that the entire Christian life is an invitation to walk with God.

> *Noah walked with God.*
>
> —Genesis 6:9 ESV

> *When Abram was ninety-nine years old the LORD appeared to Abram and said to him, "I am God Almighty; walk before me, and be blameless."*
>
> —Genesis 17:1 ESV

> *[King David prayed,] "Teach me your way, O LORD,*
> *that I may walk in your truth;*
> *unite my heart to fear your name."*
>
> —Psalm 86:11 ESV

> *This is the message we have heard from him and proclaim to you, that God is light, and in him is no darkness at all. If we say we have fellowship with him while we walk in darkness, we lie and do not practice the truth. But if we walk in the light, as he is in the light, we have fellowship with one another, and the blood of Jesus his Son cleanses us from all sin.*
>
> —1 John 1:5–7 ESV

*Walk in a manner worthy of the Lord, fully pleasing to him: bearing fruit in every good work and increasing in the knowledge of God.*

—Colossians 1:10 ESV

*For we walk by faith, not by sight.*

—2 Corinthians 5:7 ESV

Copious amounts of Scripture depict the Christian life as walking with God. For this reason, we are often described as pilgrims on a journey. We are called pilgrims because we are not home yet. As Jesus' followers, we still live in this fallen world, but we are just passing through, following Him on our journey toward our true home.

As we've seen, the grand narrative of the Bible tells us that God is bringing us back into His Presence, where we will live for eternity. Therefore, Jesus made this bold statement when the first followers of Christ asked to know the way back to God:

*I am the way, and the truth, and the life. No one comes to the Father except through me.*

—John 14:6 ESV

Jesus is not just a way back to God; He is "the Way." Friend, there is only one path home. Which is why the early Church was described as "the Way" (Acts 9:2 ESV). Those believers understood something that I think we miss today. We are followers of the One who is "the Way," and we are meant to point others to "the Way" back to God.

Jesus also made clear that this journey of walking with Him would be on the "narrow road" (see Matt. 7:13–14). There are other roads that others clamor to, but they don't lead to home. The Way is opened to us by God's amazing grace. But don't assume for a second that the journey of walking with God is without challenges!

Along our journey, we face temptations to detour from the path of righteousness (see Matt. 6:13). We encounter a real spiritual Enemy who wants to keep us from enjoying and glorifying God (see Eph. 6:10–13). And we suffer and endure hardships in this broken world (see John 16:33).

The beautiful reality of this journey is that we are not alone; God is with us—Emmanuel is our guide. Jesus is our Savior and our Friend. His Holy Spirit is our Helper and Counselor. And the Word of God is the light unto our path.

The Bible is filled with analogies to describe God's Presence with us. But one of the strongest metaphors Jesus used to describe our relationship with Him was that of sheep and a shepherd (see John 10:1–18). We shouldn't rush to take this as a compliment. Sheep are notoriously helpless creatures. They need a shepherd to guide them to water, defend them from predators, find pastures for grazing, pick them up when they fall, and heal them when they get sick. So of all the ways that Jesus could have described what it looks like for us to follow Him, He said, "I am the good shepherd; I know my sheep and my sheep know me" (John 10:14 NIV). Between sheep and their shepherd is a relationship of total dependence, but in that reliance there is one who is devoted to the care and well-being of the flock.

Friend, Jesus is your Good Shepherd.

He is with you, leading, providing, and guiding you on the journey to your eternal home. The longer we walk with Him, the more we comprehend the profound truths written long ago by another shepherd, King David. Savor this beloved psalm and soak in the reality that as you follow Jesus, it is the Lord's goodness and His mercy that lead you as you journey home.

*The LORD is my shepherd; I shall not want.*
*He makes me lie down in green pastures.*
*He leads me beside still waters.*
*He restores my soul.*
*He leads me in paths of righteousness for his name's sake…*
*Surely goodness and mercy shall follow me*
*all the days of my life,*
*and I shall dwell in the house of the LORD*
*forever.*

—Psalm 23:1–3, 6 ESV

## HARVEST

Jesus said, "I am the good shepherd; I know my sheep and my sheep know me" (John 10:14 NIV). Do you feel as if you *know* Jesus as a Shepherd who guides, provides, heals, helps, and rescues you? Take a minute to slowly pray through Psalm 23 and as you do, imagine yourself walking day by day with Jesus. As you pray, invite the Lord to restore your soul and lead you in paths of righteousness.

DAY 29

# THE BLESSED HOPE

## SEED

*For the grace of God has appeared, bringing salvation for all people, training us to renounce ungodliness and worldly passions, and to live self-controlled, upright, and godly lives in the present age,* **waiting for our blessed hope***, the appearing of the glory of our great God and Savior Jesus Christ, who gave himself for us to redeem us from all lawlessness and to purify for himself a people for his own possession who are zealous for good works.*

—Titus 2:11–14 ESV (emphasis added)

## CULTIVATE

Read Matthew 24; Revelation 19.

## FLOURISH

December 7, 1941, is a day that "lives in infamy." These are the famous words President Franklin D. Roosevelt used to describe the Japanese attack on American forces at Pearl Harbor. This brutal event propelled the United States to join the Allied forces in World War II.

Within hours of the raid on Pearl Harbor, the Japanese turned their attention to the Philippines, another pivotal island in the Pacific. Thousands of American troops were stationed there, but the US could not adequately defend the island because its naval fleet had been severely disabled in the attack on Pearl Harbor. Despite insufficient supplies, American and Filipino troops held their ground for three months, but in early March 1942, the Japanese bottled up the US forces on the Bataan Peninsula. A few weeks later, the United States surrendered the Philippines to Japan.

The remaining troops were forced into the infamous Bataan Death March—a sixty-five-mile slog across the peninsula to a prisoner of war camp. Thousands died as the Japanese forces committed some of the most horrific war crimes ever known.

This fateful event is dear to my family because my husband's great-grandfather, Ralph Ellis, was one of the American troops left on Bataan. He survived the brutal death march and became a prisoner of war. By God's grace, he was one of the surviving POWs rescued near the war's end. It baffles the mind to consider the atrocities these soldiers faced—beatings, starvation, disease, and psychological torture. Yet, day after day, they endured the darkness because of their hope. Their hope was in the promised return of their leader, General Douglas MacArthur.

One month before Bataan fell to the Japanese forces, President Roosevelt ordered General MacArthur to leave the island. Since MacArthur grew up in the Philippines as a boy, he was personally connected to the people. And as a military commander, he was devoted to his soldiers. The last thing MacArthur wanted to do was evacuate, and he planned to share the same fate as the troops. Therefore, it took a direct order from the president to force MacArthur to leave.

General MacArthur barely escaped, and as he sailed away, he made a famous vow: "I shall return!"[1] His solemn oath to return became the beacon of hope for those suffering on the embattled island. The Filipino people radio-broadcasted MacArthur's speech, and it was heard by frightened children, their parents, American POWs, and even their captors. I imagine the weary and beaten-down soldiers encouraged one another with this promise.

It was nearly three years later, on October 22, 1944, when General MacArthur stood on Philippine soil and declared, "I have returned!"[2] The photo of him wading through the Pacific Ocean and stepping onshore is one of the most iconic images of World War II. His first step onto enemy-occupied territory shows the fulfillment of a promise and the culmination of years of waiting as he liberated the island from the grip of Japanese forces.

This historic event captures my heart because it perfectly illustrates the world in which we live. As followers of Jesus Christ, we are not home yet. We, too, live in enemy-occupied territory. To the followers of Christ in Ephesus, the apostle Paul shared this sobering reality:

> *Finally, be strong in the Lord and in the strength of his might. Put on the whole armor of God, that you may be able to stand against the schemes of the devil. For we do not wrestle against flesh and blood, but against the rulers, against the authorities, against the cosmic powers over this present darkness, against the spiritual forces of evil in the heavenly places.*
>
> —Ephesians 6:10–12 ESV

---

1 Peter Eisner, "Without Chick Parsons, General MacArthur May Never Have Made His Famed Return to the Philippines," *Smithsonian Magazine*, September 2017, https://www.smithsonianmag.com/history/without-chick-parsons-General-MacArthur-Never-Made-Return-Philippines-180964406/.

2 Ibid.

This world is a war zone where the evil one rules over the realm of darkness, and we await the glorious return of King Jesus, who promises to deliver His Church.

Two thousand years ago, Jesus won the battle over sin and death on the cross, but the final victory is still to come when He will destroy Satan and his forces of darkness forever. When Jesus prepared the disciples for His departure, He gave this promise:

> *And if I go and prepare a place for you, I will come again and will take you to myself, that where I am you may be also.*
>
> —John 14:3 ESV

When Jesus ascended to heaven (see Acts 1:1–11), He left earth to go prepare a place for us, and He promised to return. Jesus Christ's return to vanquish the Enemy and deliver His people is the blessed hope of the Church (see Titus 2:11–14). While we are explicitly told we can't know when He will return, we are repeatedly promised that it will happen. The Bible says:

> *This Jesus, who was taken up from you into heaven, will come in the same way as you saw him go into heaven.*
>
> —Acts 1:11 ESV

> *Behold, he is coming with the clouds, and every eye will see him.*
>
> —Revelation 1:7 ESV

> *When the Son of Man comes in his glory, and all the angels with him, then he will sit on his glorious throne.*
>
> —Matthew 25:31 ESV

As we've seen in our survey of the Bible from garden to garden, God's track record on keeping His promises is 100 percent. The return of Jesus Christ will be the greatest event in all of human history. Every eye will see Him as He splits open heaven and descends with His angelic army and stands on earth as the King of Glory. We await His return with joyful expectation, knowing that He lingers so that more and more people can place their faith in Him and be delivered from the Day of Judgment.

While some speculate, developing elaborate timetables about Christ's return, the Bible clearly says we should not theorize, but simply be ready for Him. We are a bride waiting for the arrival of her Groom. We are to walk through these days loving Him and living in holy expectation for when our Redeemer will rescue us and make all things new. We live in this world remembering that this is not our home but awaiting the One who will take us there. This, my friend, is our blessed hope.

> *For the Lord himself will descend from heaven with a cry of command, with the voice of an archangel, and with the sound of the trumpet of God. And the dead in Christ will rise first. Then we who are alive, who are left, will be caught up together with them in the clouds to meet the Lord in the air, and so we will always be with the Lord.*
>
> —1 Thessalonians 4:16–17 ESV

## HARVEST

God's Word tells us that He "desires all people to be saved and to come to the knowledge of the truth" (1 Tim. 2:4 ESV). As we await the promised return of Christ, we can share the Good News of the Gospel with those around us who don't know Him! Who are the people in your life who need to know this blessed hope? Take a moment to pray for each person by name.

## DAY 30

# THE NEW CREATION

### SEED

*Then I saw a new heaven and a new earth, for the first heaven and the first earth had passed away, and the sea was no more. And I saw the holy city, new Jerusalem, coming down out of heaven from God, prepared as a bride adorned for her husband. And I heard a loud voice from the throne saying, "Behold, the dwelling place of God is with man. He will dwell with them, and they will be his people, and God himself will be with them as their God. He will wipe away every tear from their eyes, and death shall be no more, neither shall there be mourning, nor crying, nor pain anymore, for the former things have passed away." And he who was seated on the throne said, "Behold, I am making all things new." Also he said, "Write this down, for these words are trustworthy and true."*

—Revelation 21:1–5 ESV

### CULTIVATE

Read Revelation 21–22.

### FLOURISH

The Bible is the epic story revealing the Author of Life, the creation of the world, the glorious design of humanity, and the tragic fall of God's image-bearers into sin. But the Bible doesn't end with explaining the bad news of what happened to us. Instead, in a gracious act of love, God's Word serves as our light in the midst of darkness, pointing us to the hope in this dark world.

That hope is centered on the Redeemer, the "Seed of the woman." The One promised in Eden who would restore all things by crushing the Serpent, the father of lies and ruler of the darkness. As the story unfolds, we discover that this promised Seed is the very Son of God. Jesus Christ came to earth as one of us, lived a perfect life, and died in our place so that those who place faith in Him can become children of God (see John 3:16).

Only God could write this story; every detail points to His Divine Authorship. The salvation story alone is mind-blowing, but the Bible doesn't stop there. For God's plan for all eternity has been to dwell with His people. Genesis reveals God's original design was for us to live with Him in face-to-face friendship. Complete restoration brings God's children back into His Presence, back to an Edenic state, where we live with Him for eternity.

Tim Keller notes:

> When we look at the whole scope of this story line, we see clearly that Christianity is not only about getting one's individual sins forgiven so we can go to heaven. That is an important means of God's salvation, but not the final end or purpose of it. The purpose of Jesus's coming is to put the whole world right, to renew and restore the creation.[1]

All great stories have a beginning, a middle, and an end. The opening tells us how the drama started. The middle explains the road traveled along the way. And an ending reveals the dramatic resolution. In a classic Western, we cheer as the cowboy rides away

1 Keller, *Reason for God*, 223.

victorious. In a romantic comedy, we cry when the torn-apart couple embraces. In an action thriller, we breathe a sigh of relief when the hero renders justice.

The Bible is the God-breathed redemption story that tells the past, the present, and the glorious future awaiting the children of God. As we've journeyed from garden to garden, we've seen this drama unfold, leading us to the important question: How will this story end?

> *He who has an ear, let him hear what the Spirit says to the churches. To the one who conquers I will grant to eat of the tree of life, which is in the paradise of God.*
>
> —Revelation 2:7 ESV

The book of Revelation shows us that God's redemptive work through His Son will culminate when He makes all things new! The people of God are once again granted to eat of the Tree of Life, the curse of the fall is broken, and life in Eden is restored! There will be a new heaven and earth, and the Lord God Almighty will once again dwell with His people, forever!

In the words of Randy Alcorn,

> When God walked with Adam and Eve in the Garden, Earth was Heaven's backyard. The New Earth will be even more than that—it will be Heaven itself. And those who know Jesus will have the privilege of living there.[2]

Jesus is called our Redeemer, for that is precisely what He does. He takes the broken and makes us beautiful. He takes the sick and makes us whole. He takes the empty and gives us fullness. He is the great restorer of all things. We discover in Revelation a great

2 Alcorn, *Heaven*, 103.

reversal—the Lord will right every wrong, wipe away every tear, destroy the evil one, and restore all that was lost.

This truth is a healing balm for the suffering soul. In this broken world where children die, where sickness ravages bodies, and sin tears apart families, we have this blessed hope—our God will make all things new and wipe away every tear from our eyes. Our comfort in this sin-stained world is not in trying to make heaven on earth, but in the fact that the Lord Jesus Christ will return victorious and reign unrivaled on a New Earth where sin, suffering, sickness, and sorrow will never enter.

I pray you'll take time to savor the CULTIVATE (Revelation 21–22) passages today and marvel at the completeness of the Bible. The similarities to Eden in the New Creation are striking—the river and the Tree of Life, but most importantly, the Presence of God.

> *Then the angel showed me the river of the water of life, bright as crystal, flowing from the throne of God and of the Lamb through the middle of the street of the city; also, on either side of the river, the tree of life with its twelve kinds of fruit, yielding its fruit each month. The leaves of the tree were for the healing of the nations. No longer will there be anything accursed, but the throne of God and of the Lamb will be in it, and his servants will worship him. They will see his face, and his name will be on their foreheads.*
>
> —Revelation 22:1–4 ESV

The apostle John stretched the limits of human vocabulary to describe what he beheld. He tried to articulate the splendor but was left using phrases such as "It is like this" to describe God's magnificent future for us. Which is why the apostle Paul tells us:

*No eye has seen, no ear has heard,*
*and no mind has imagined*
*what God has prepared*
*for those who love him.*

—1 Corinthians 2:9 NLT

For those with an image of a dull heavenly state where one floats on a cloud playing a harp, the book of Revelation puts a quick end to such nonsense. Instead, we will be the redeemed people of God inhabiting a New Earth, blissfully untainted by sin. Imagine the best this world offers in beauty, food, or pleasure, and then magnify that by infinity.

We will inhabit new bodies free from corruption, cancer, sickness, disease, and death—forever! Friend, fear not—we will not be bored on the New Earth because we will fulfill the purpose we were created for, using our gifts, talents, and intellect to glorify God for all eternity.

Says Randy Alcorn,

> In Genesis, God plants the Garden on Earth; in Revelation, he brings down the New Jerusalem, with a garden at its center, to the New Earth. In Eden, there's no sin, death, or Curse; on the New Earth, there's no more sin, death, or Curse. In Genesis, the Redeemer is promised; in Revelation, the Redeemer returns. Genesis tells the story of Paradise lost; Revelation tells the story of Paradise regained.
>
> In Genesis, humanity's stewardship is squandered; in Revelation, humanity's stewardship is triumphant, empowered by the human and divine King Jesus. These parallels are too remarkable to be anything but deliberate. These mirror images demonstrate the perfect symmetry of God's

plan. We live in the in-between time, hearing echoes of Eden and the approaching footfalls of the New Earth.[3]

Friend, as we conclude this journey from garden to garden, hear the One who spoke the stars into orbit, who formed you in your mother's womb, and who moved heaven and earth to redeem you, make you this glorious promise:

> *And the one sitting on the throne said, "Look, I am making everything new!" And then he said to me, "Write this down, for what I tell you is trustworthy and true."*
>
> —Revelation 21:5 NLT

## HARVEST

Oh, my friend, I hope you share the joy that I have as I ponder God's promise of our glorious eternity with Him! It is just too great for us to comprehend! I pray you hold fast to His Word and His promises. May we walk with Jesus in such a way that our broken and dark world sees His light and turns toward Him. Take time to praise God for His heart to redeem and restore all things. Ask the Lord to increase your hunger for His Presence and your passion to live for His glory.

---

3 Alcorn, *Heaven*, 85.

# ACKNOWLEDGMENTS

In many ways writing *Garden to Garden* is my life's work, and this journey through God's Word has been an absolute labor of love. Looking back over twenty-five years of following Jesus, I marvel at how the Lord used countless teachers, mentors, and life experiences to pour a Christ-centered theology and love for Scripture into me.

I owe a huge debt of gratitude to the men and women, all extraordinary Bible teachers, who helped me see Jesus as the unrivaled Star of the story: Dr. Ed Young, Dr. Ben Young, Dr. Jim DeLoach, Louie Giglio, Beth Moore, Matt Surber, and Dr. Jim Hamilton. And as the reader will probably note, the writings of A. W. Tozer, C. S. Lewis, Tim Keller, and Randy Alcorn greatly influenced *Garden to Garden*.

I would like to thank my home church, Mission City Church in San Antonio, Texas, for the honor of teaching women the Word of God. Serving alongside you to reach our city for Christ and see lives transformed by the Gospel is an absolute gift.

I want to thank my agent, Whitney Gossett of Content Capital, for her consistent encouragement and championship of this book. I'm forever grateful for the publishing and marketing teams at Hachette Book Group, especially the tremendous guidance and direction from Daisy Hutton, Kathryn Riggs, and Abigail Skinner. This book is far better because of the wisdom and care you added.

*Garden to Garden* would not be a reality without the help of my friend Sarah Thompson. Your editorial feedback and crafting of the HARVEST questions (while homeschooling three kids) made this book a reality. In addition, I am blessed by the faithful prayer covering of the *This Redeemed Life* Ministry board of directors and for the incredible support of friends and coworkers at Mission City Church San Antonio.

Finally, I want to thank my family.

Mom and Dad, thank you for passing on a love for God and His Word to your children.

Andrew, Brenden, and Sydney: You are the best kids I could ever ask for and always the first to read anything I write. Thank you for the love and support and for dealing with my deadlines.

Justin, my beloved husband and ministry partner...what a ride!! Only God could write our story, and I'm so thankful He did!

# *GARDEN TO GARDEN* SMALL-GROUP RESOURCES

To access additional resources for ***Garden to Garden***, visit:

www.thisredeemedlife.org/gardentogarden

- (6) 30-minute Bible teaching videos featuring Marian Jordan Ellis
- Small-Group Discussion Questions
- *Garden to Garden* Lent 40-Day Reading Plan

# ABOUT THE AUTHOR

**Marian Jordan Ellis** is a Bible teacher with an evangelist's heart who is passionate about Jesus and helping women experience the victorious Christian life. She holds a master's degree in Biblical Studies from Southwestern Baptist Theological Seminary. Marian teaches a monthly gathering (TueGather) in San Antonio, Texas, at Mission City Church, where she serves as the director of Women's Ministry. (These teachings can be found on YouTube @thisredeemedlife or the TRL App.)

Marian's powerful redemption testimony and her dynamic account of the grace of Christ that radically transformed her life permeates all of her writings and speaking engagements. She's whole in Christ and ready to tell any ear that will listen! She's the author of numerous books for women. Her Bible study, *For His Glory: Living as God's Masterpiece*, is a verse-by-verse study of Ephesians.

Marian and her husband, Justin, live in San Antonio, and they have three children: Andrew, Brenden, and Sydney.